CLASSIC SERMONS ON DEATH AND DYING

The Kregel Classic Sermons Series

Angels
Apostle Paul
Apostle Peter
Attributes of God
Birth of Christ
Christian Service
Church
Cross of Christ
Death and Dying
Faith and Doubt
Family and Home
Grace of God
Heaven and Hell
Holy Spirit
Hope
Judas Iscariot
Lesser-Known Bible Characters
Lord's Prayer
Love of God
Miracles of Jesus
Names of God
Old Testament Prophets
Overcoming Fear
Parables of Jesus
Praise
Prayer
Prodigal Son
Resurrection of Christ
Revival and Spiritual Renewal
Seasons of Life
Second Coming/Prophetic Themes
Sovereignty of God
Spiritual Warfare
Stewardship
Suffering
Will of God
Word of God
World Evangelism
Worship

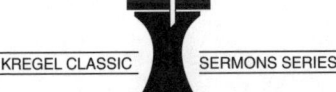

KREGEL CLASSIC SERMONS SERIES

CLASSIC SERMONS ON DEATH AND DYING

**Compiled by
Warren W. Wiersbe**

Grand Rapids, MI 49501

Classic Sermons on Death and Dying
Compiled by Warren W. Wiersbe

© 2000 by Kregel Publications. All rights reserved. No part of this book may be reproduced, stored in a retrieval system, or transmitted in any form or by any means—electronic, mechanical, photocopy, recording, or otherwise—without written permission of the publisher, except for brief quotations in printed reviews.

Published by Kregel Publications, a division of Kregel, Inc., P.O. Box 2607, Grand Rapids, MI 49501. Kregel Publications provides trusted, biblical publications for Christian growth and service. Your comments and suggestions are valued.

Scripture used by permission of Thomas Nelson, Inc., original publisher of the American Standard Version.

For more information about Kregel Publications, visit our web site at: www.kregel.com

Cover photo: PhotoDisc

Library of Congress Cataloging-in-Publication Data
Classic sermons on death and dying / Warren W. Wiersbe, compiler.
    p.   cm.— (Kregel classic sermons series)
ISBN 0-8254-4150-1

Printed in the United States of America
1 2 3 4 5 / 04 03 02 01 00

Contents

List of Scripture Texts 6
Preface 7
1. Death, a Sleep 9
   Charles Haddon Spurgeon
2. The Village Tragedy 27
   Clovis Gillham Chappell
3. A Prisoner's Dying Thoughts 37
   Alexander Maclaren
4. The Days of Our Years 49
   Joseph Parker
5. The Sorrows of the Bereaved Spread
   Before Jesus 59
   Jonathan Edwards
6. Christ's Delay to Interpose Against Death 75
   John Ker
7. Death of Stephen 89
   Robert Murray McCheyne
8. Victory Over Death 99
   Frederick W. Robertson
9. The Inevitable Word 115
   Clarence Edward Noble Macartney
10. Christ and the Fear of Death 125
    George H. Morrison
11. The Shortness of Life 133
    Phillips Brooks
12. The Vanquished Enemy 149
    George Campbell Morgan

List of Scripture Texts

Psalm 90:10, Parker 49
Matthew 14:12, Edwards 59
John 11:14, Chappell 27
John 11:32, Ker 75
Acts 7:59, McCheyne 89
1 Corinthians 7:29, Brooks 133
1 Corinthians 15:26, Morgan 149
1 Corinthians 15:56-57, Robertson 99
1 Thessalonians 4:13, Spurgeon 9
2 Timothy 4:6-8, Maclaren 37
Hebrews 2:15, Morrison 125
Hebrews 9:27, Macartney 115

Preface

THE *Kregel Classic Sermons Series* is an attempt to assemble and publish meaningful sermons from master preachers about significant themes.

These are *sermons*, not essays or chapters taken from books about themes. Not all of these sermons could be called great, but all of them are *meaningful*. They apply the truths of the Bible to the needs of the human heart, which is something that all effective preaching must do.

While some are better known than others, all of the preachers whose sermons I have selected had important ministries and were highly respected in their day. The fact that a sermon is included in this volume does not mean that either the compiler or the publisher agrees with or endorses everything that the man did, preached, or wrote. The sermon is here because it has a valued contribution to make.

These are sermons about *significant* themes. The pulpit is no place to play with trivia. The preacher has thirty minutes in which to help mend broken hearts, change defeated lives, and save lost souls; he can never accomplish this demanding ministry by distributing homiletical tidbits. In these difficult days we do not need clever pulpiteers who discuss the times; we need dedicated ambassadors who will preach the eternities.

The reading of these sermons can enrich your spiritual life. The studying of them can enrich your skills as an interpreter and expounder of God's truth. However God uses these sermons in your life and ministry, my prayer is that His church around the world will be encouraged and strengthened by them.

—WARREN W. WIERSBE

Death, a Sleep

Charles Haddon Spurgeon (1834–1892) is undoubtedly the most famous minister of the nineteenth century. Converted in 1850, he united with the Baptists and soon began to preach in various places. He became pastor of the Baptist church in Waterbeach, England, in 1851, and three years later he was called to the decaying Park Street Church, London. Within a short time the work began to prosper, a new church was built and dedicated in 1861, and Spurgeon became London's most popular preacher. In 1855, he began to publish his sermons weekly; today they make up the fifty-seven volumes of *The Metropolitan Tabernacle Pulpit*. He founded a pastor's college and several orphanages.

This sermon was taken from *The Metropolitan Tabernacle Pulpit,* volume 54 for 1908.

1

Death, a Sleep

> But I would not have you to be ignorant, brethren, concerning them which are asleep, that ye sorrow not, even as others which have no hope. (1 Thessalonians 4:13)

THERE MAY BE SOME few extraordinary cases where "ignorance is bliss," and where "'tis folly to be wise." But, for the most part, ignorance is the mother of misery, and if we had more knowledge, we should find it a tower of strength against many fears and alarms that beget sadness and sorrows in dark untutored minds. True it is that the utmost diligence of the student cannot shield his body or his mind from fatigue and distress. In guarding against one class of ills, we may become exposed to another, as Solomon testifies that "much study is a weariness of the flesh" (Eccl. 12:12), and again, "in much wisdom is much grief: and he that increaseth knowledge increaseth sorrow" (1:18). Still, be it remembered that "wisdom is a defense, and money is a defense;" in the increase of either we may augment our cares, yet in the increase of both we think there is a remunerative profit.

But I would commend to you a wisdom which springs not up from earth, but comes down from heaven. He that is rich toward God knows that "the blessing of the LORD, it maketh rich, and he addeth no sorrow with it" (Prov. 10:22), and he that is made wise to salvation has received that wisdom which "giveth life to them that have it" (Eccl. 7:12). If we had more celestial wisdom, I believe we should have more of heavenly joy and less of carnal sorrow. Many a doctrine of the gospel becomes the means of sadness and misery to the heart simply because it is not understood. Ignorance of the Bible often troubles men's hearts and consciences and prevents them from finding that peace of God which a little more knowledge of it would be sure to give them. And I am certain that ignorance or forgetfulness of many of the exceedingly great and precious promises of God, and of the marvelous things He has engaged to do for His people, often causes our eyes to flow with tears and our hearts to be overwhelmed with suffering. The more a Christian knows of his religion, the better for his peace and for his happiness. The apostle says, "I would not have you to be ignorant, brethren." *He* knew that was an ill condition, and *we* may well shun it. Depend upon this: the more thoroughly you understand the gospel, the more you will find that the gospel blesses you and makes you happy. Each word that Eternal Wisdom speaks is pure. Give heed then to the sure word of Scripture so you shall journey as with chart in hand, escaping a thousand dangers to which benighted travelers are exposed, and enjoying a thousand delights which they cannot discern. But alas for those who walk in darkness! They have nothing to cheer or enliven, but everything to frighten and terrify them.

Leaving this preliminary point, for I trust you seek to avoid all ignorance and ask God to lead you into the knowledge of all truth, I proceed now to the special application of my text, as the Holy Spirit has designed to place a lamp in the sepulcher where darkness was wont to hold an undisputed sway. And here we have, first, *an affecting metaphor*—a metaphor for death: "them which are asleep." Secondly, there is *a solemn distinction.* There are some that die without hope, and there are others for whom we sorrow not as for them that are without hope. Then, thirdly, there is *a very gentle exhortation*—not to sorrow for them that sleep in Jesus, "even as others which have no hope."

A Most Affecting Simile: "Them Which Are Asleep"

Scripture continually uses the term "sleep" to express death. Our Savior did so. He said, "Our friend Lazarus sleepeth" (John 11:11). And so well, with such an evident and appropriate truthfulness, did he describe death as being a sleep, that his disciples mistook the sense of his words, and said, "Lord, if he sleep, he shall do well" (v. 12). But Jesus spoke not of the transient sleep of the weary, but of the deep slumber of death. Very frequently, even in the Old Testament, you find it said that certain persons "slept with their fathers; and were buried in a sepulcher." Nor did they count that sleep a hopeless end of life. But as David said "I shall be satisfied, when I awake, with thy likeness" (Ps. 17:15), they expected to awake from that slumber into which they believed death did cast their bodies. In the New Testament the same emblem is continually used, and it is very pleasant to remember that in the old catacombs of Rome, where the bodies of many saints were buried, it is continually found inscribed on their graves, "She sleeps," "He sleeps in Jesus," "He shall wake up one day;" and similar epitaphs, which mark the firm belief of Christians that sleep was a very fine and beautiful picture of death.

Allow me to guard against an evil supposition that may spring up here. When death is called a sleep, it is not because the soul sleeps. The soul, we are told by Holy Scripture, rises at once to heaven. The soul of the saint is found at once before the throne of God. It is the body that is said to sleep. The soul sleeps not. Absent from the body, the soul is present with the Lord. It stretches its wings and flies away up to yonder realm of joy. There, reveling in delight, bathing itself in bliss, it finds a rest from the turmoil of earth infinitely better than any rest in sleep. It is the body, then, that sleeps, and the body only. I will try and tell you why we think the metaphor is used of the sleep of the body.

In the first place, because *sleep is a suspension of the faculties, but not a destruction of the body*. When we see anyone naturally asleep, we believe that body will wake up again. We do not suppose that those eyes will be sealed up in perpetual darkness, that those bones and that flesh will lie dormant never more to feel the consciousness of being, or stir with the impulse of life. No, we expect to see the functions of life resumed, the eyelids open to admit the cheering rays of light, and the limbs to become again exercised with activity. So, when we bury our dead in our graves, we are taught to believe that they are asleep. Our faith (which is warranted by the Word of God) discerns in the corruption of death a suspension of the powers of the body rather than an annihilation of the matter itself. The earthly house of this tabernacle must be dissolved, but it cannot be destroyed. Though the bones be scattered to the four winds of heaven, yet, at the call of the Lord God, they shall come together again, bone to his bone. Though the eyes be first glazed and then devoured from their sockets, they shall be surely restored, that each saint in his own flesh may see God.

In this confidence we deposit the body of each departed saint in the grave as in a bed. We doubt not that God will guard the dust of the precious sons and daughters of Zion. We believe that in the resurrection there shall be a perfect identity of the body. You may call it unphilosophical if you please, but you cannot show me that it is unbiblical. Science cannot demonstrate it, you say; but then science cannot disprove it. Reason stands abashed, while Revelation lifts her trumpet-tongue and exclaims, "Behold, I show you a mystery; We shall not all sleep, but we shall all be changed, in a moment, in the twinkling of an eye, at the last trump: for the trumpet shall sound, and the dead shall be raised incorruptible" (1 Cor. 15:51–52).

Look not, then, on the corpse of your brother or your sister in Christ, beloved, to take an eternal farewell. Say rather, "When I stretch myself on my couch at night, I *hope* to wake at the first call of busy morn. But I not only hope, I *am sure*, that this sleeping heir of immortality shall awake from the sound slumbers of his sepulchral repose at the dawn of the heavenly Bridegroom's appearing." "Ah!" says one, "'twas but an hour or two ago I was in the closed chamber where my little baby is laid out. I lifted the coffin lid and looked at its dear little placid face. I can quite believe what you say. Death is a sleep; it seemed just like it." "No," says another, "it was only yesterday that I was in a London graveyard, appalled with the sight of skulls and bare, disjointed bones. I can never look upon death in the way you represent." Now then, my friends, mark this well, for I can give one reply to you both. It is not by the exercise of your sense, but by the exercise of your faith, that you are to get this blessed hope. You might bitterly gaze on the face of the dead long enough before you would catch a symptom of returning life; you might grope about in the dark damp vault long enough before a ray of light would show you an avenue by which the captives can be liberated from their gloomy cells. No, no; you must visit the tomb of Jesus. You must go and "see the place where the Lord lay" (Matt. 28:6), then you will soon perceive how the stone is rolled away, and how to rise again is made possible and certain, too.

Moreover, *the term "sleep" is beautifully used to express the quiet of the body.* It rests from labor. Look on the sleeper. He has been weary. He has toiled all day long, but there is no weariness now. He breathes softly. Sometimes a dream may disturb him, but he is not weary. He is resting in the unconsciousness of slumber. It is often pleasing to look upon the face of a weary sleeper. Have you never passed along a country lane, and there by the roadside seen the harvest man as he is resting awhile from his toils, lying down upon the bank? What a heavy sleep he has, and what a blessed smile there is on his countenance while he is enjoying that rest! Such is the natural sleep of the body, whence comes the metaphor of my text. Is not this sleep of death a resting after toil? The poor limbs are weary. They are now stretched in the grave and covered over with the green sod that they may not hear the noise above their heads nor be disturbed by the busy din. They are put in their quiet abodes down deep there in the earth that none may alarm them. Now let the cannon roar over their tomb, let the thunder shake the sky, let the lightning flash; no sight nor sound can startle them or cause them dreams. In such still chambers of retirement their troubles now are over. "There the wicked cease from troubling; and there the weary be at rest" (Job 3:17). The body has gone through its battle. The warrior sleeps, the conqueror rests, his brow shall soon be decked with laurels. The very brow that now slumbers in the tomb awhile shall yet rise again to wear the crown of everlasting life. But now it rests awhile until the preparations are complete for the triumphant entry into the kingdom of God, when Christ shall come to receive body and soul into their everlasting resting place.

Note again, *sleep is used as a figure for death to show us the entire unconcern which the dead feel concerning anything that is going on below.* The sleeper knows nothing of what is doing. The thief may be in the house, but he knows it not. There is a storm, but he slumbers and knows no terror. There may happen a thousand accidents abroad, or even in the chamber where he rests, but, so long as sleep can hold him fast, he shall be entirely unconcerned about them and shall not notice them. And such, beloved, is the case with the dead. Their bodies, at least, are entirely free from concern. Empires may totter, kingdoms fall, and mighty revolutions shake the world, but none of these things will

> Ever make their hearts to ache, or
> Break the spell of their profound repose.

There may be a falling away, a backsliding, in the church, but the minister in the grave knows it not. The tongue of Wycliffe shall not move with stern rebuke; the eye of Knox shall not flash with indignation. Yea, and each bodily organ through which the mind was wont to reveal itself is now closed: "So man lieth down, and riseth not: till the heavens be no more, they shall not awake, nor be raised out of their sleep" (Job 14:12).

There is a yet sweeter view of this metaphor which I will now point out to you. *Sleep,* you know, *is a means of refreshment,* by the recruiting of our exhausted strength to fit us for a fresh exercise of our faculties when we awake. Such, too, is death. The sleep of death is requisite as a preparation for heaven, so far as the body is concerned. The soul must be prepared by a blessed change wrought upon it in this time-state. But the body awaits its full redemption until the resurrection. Though I may not follow the metaphor in the process by which the change is wrought, I can believe it will quite hold good in the result. The refreshing of the body is, of course, gradually brought about during the hours of sleep, just as changes are successively going on in the grain of wheat that falls into the ground and dies. The awaking of the one and the sprouting of the other, in health and vigor, result from causes that take place in the interval. But I am not prepared to say that it is exactly so with the sleeping dust of man's earthly tabernacle. The greedy worm that devours it, the general corruption that preys upon it, and the foul earth with which it mingles may consume that which is corruptible, but these can have no power to refine the nature or to produce the glorious likeness to be borne by the saints. You must always guard against straining a figure, especially when, by so doing, you would make it contradict the plain didactic teachings of the Scriptures. We do not look down into the grave as if it were a refining pot to purify our nature, or a bath in which the garments of mortality are to be cleansed. But we look upward to heaven from whence the Savior shall come, our "Lord Jesus Christ: who shall change our vile body, that it may be fashioned like unto his glorious body, according to the working whereby he is able even to subdue all things unto himself" (Phil. 3:20-21).

Once more, there is a very precious word in connection with this sleep which we must not overlook. At the fourteenth verse it says that they "sleep in Jesus." Sweet thought! This teaches us that death does not dissolve the union which subsists between the believer and Christ. When the body dies, it does not cease to be a part of Christ. "Know ye not that your bodies are the members of Christ?" (1 Cor. 6:15), said the apostle to those who were still living in the world. Now, as to those whose earthly course is done, our departed friends "sleep in Jesus." They are as much in Christ now as they were when upon earth. Their bodies, which were precious to the Lord and preserved as the apple of His eye, are as precious to Him now as ever they were. It was once their delight to have communion with Jesus in His death and resurrection, as knowing themselves one with Him when He died and rose again. Not less surely did Jesus hold fellowship with them in *their* death, making Himself known to them when they endured their last struggle. How often have we seen the eye brighten up with an almost supernatural brilliance just before it was closed on all beneath the skies! How often have we seen the hand raised with the parting expression of triumph and then laid motionless by the side! How often has the presence of the Beloved sustained the frail tenement of the expiring Christian until he has defied death "to quench his immortality, or shake his trust in God!"

And mark how the saints in Jesus, when their bodies sleep in peace, have perpetual fellowship with Him—aye, better fellowship than we can enjoy. We have but the transitory glimpse of His face; they gaze upon it every moment. We see Him "through a glass, darkly"; they behold Him "face to face" (1 Cor. 13:12). We sip of the brook by the way; they plunge into the very ocean of unbounded love. We look up sometimes and see our Father smile; look whenever they may, His face is always full of smiles for them. We get some drops of comfort; but they get the honeycomb itself. They have their cup filled with new wine, running over with perennial, unalloyed delights. They are full of peace and joy forever. They "sleep in Jesus."

Beloved, such a description of death makes us wish to sleep, too. O Lord, let us go to sleep with the departed! O happy hour when a clod of the valley shall be our pillow! Though it be so hard, we shall not be affected by it. Happy hour, when earth shall be our bed! Cold shall be the clay, but we shall not know it. We shall slumber and rest. The worm shall hold carnival within our bones, and corruption shall riot over our frame. But we shall not feel it. Corruption can but feed on the corruptible; mortality can but prey upon the mortal.

Oh, let me rest! Come, night, and let me slumber! Come, my last hour! Let me bow myself upon the bed! Come, death, oh, come lightly to my couch! Aye, strike if you will, but your stroke is the loving touch that makes my body slumber. Happy, happy, they who die in the Lord!

A Solemn Distinction

All men die, but all men die not alike. There are two sorts of death. I speak not now of the inferior animals; of them we never read in Scripture that they sleep. But I speak of *man,* concerning whom it is certain that "there shall be a resurrection of the dead, both of the just and unjust" (Acts 24:15). There is the death of the righteous, which is peaceful, happy, and joyous beyond expression in its future consequences. There is, moreover, the death of the wicked, sad in itself, but doleful indeed in its inevitable results throughout a dread eternity. Come, then, beloved, let us consider this distinction. There are some, we must infer from this text, for whom we can sorrow as those for whom we have no hope, while there are others, for whom we are told we may not thus sorrow. Concerning their death we have every hope and every joy.

Turning for a moment to the heathen nations, we do not wonder that there is a great deal of grief expressed at their funerals. They hire women who pluck their hair, make hideous noises, and distress their bodies with all kinds of unnatural contortions in order to express the utmost agony, while the relatives and friends cover themselves with sackcloth and ashes, and spend their time in weeping and wailing and lamentations. We do not wonder that such customs should prevail, and be handed down among those who have no knowledge of a resurrection. They suppose that, when the body is consigned to the tomb, they shall never see it again, so we do not marvel that they should cry,

> Weep for the dead, and bewail her;
> Weep for the dead, and bewail her:
>   She is gone; she is gone;
>   We shall see her no more;—
> Weep for the dead, and bewail her!

You see, there is no hope in their case to mitigate their woe. But, in a nominally Christian land, although we are persuaded that all men will have a resurrection, yet how many die of whom we have no hope! I mean to say, we have, in the first place, no hope of ever meeting them again. We frequently sing in our Sunday school—our little children sing—

> Oh, that will be joyful,
>   Joyful, joyful!
> When we meet to part no more!

But there is another side to that truth,

> Oh, that will be doleful,
>   Doleful, doleful!
> When we part to meet no more!

When our wicked friends die, if we are righteous, we must remember that we shall never meet them again. We may behold them, but it will be a hideous sight; we may see them as Lazarus saw the rich man in hell; or we may behold them with the great gulf fixed between us. But remember that the last shake of the hand with an ungodly relative is an everlasting farewell. That last whisper of sympathy on the dying bed is indeed final. We shall never address them with another soft word of comfort; never again shall we call them friends. We are sundered now forever. Death, like some mighty earthquake, shakes two hearts apart, which seemed to be indissolubly united, and a great gulf of fire and wrath shall separate them. One in heaven and the other in hell, they shall never meet again. There is no hope of it.

Some of you we could not bear to lose. Yet, if you fall asleep, we shall with holy assurance consign you to your grave and say, "Lord, we thank You that it has pleased You to take to Yourself our beloved brother." Yet, alas, there are many here—oh! we pray God that they may not die, for we know we should never see them again in peace and joy and happiness. There are some of you now within the reach of my voice—you judge of whom I speak—concerning whom, if you were now to depart, we might say, as David did, "O my son Absalom, my son, my son Absalom! would God I had died for thee, O Absalom, my son, my son!" (2 Sam. 18:33). If you were now to depart, we might indeed take up a very bitter cry. We might ask the owl and the bittern, with their dismal hootings, to assist our lamentations. We should have need to weep for you, not because your bodies were dead, but because your souls were cast away into unutterable torment. O, if some of you were to die, it would be your mother's grief, for she would bitterly reflect that you were gnashing your teeth in fell despair. She would recollect that you were beyond the reach of prayer, cast away from all hope and from all refuge. She would recollect that she could never see you again—her destiny to be forever with her Lord in heaven, but your doom to be forever shut out!

Young men and women, and all of you who have had pious friends who have gone before, would you not like to meet them before the eternal throne? Can you bear the dread thought that you are separated from some of them forever because you are not the Lord's children, neither do you seek the things that belong to your peace? I think you wish to meet them there; do you not? But you never shall except you tread the steps they trod and walk the road they loved. If your hearts are not toward Jesus, if your souls are not given to Him, how can you? For if your way be not the same, your ends must differ. You shall not meet at the goal of heaven unless you meet at the wicket-gate on earth and enter in by the strait gate and go along the strait and narrow road. Oh, if some of you were about to die, your minister would have to go to your bedside and say, "Adieu, I shall never see you anymore." Were you to look up and say, "What, sir, no more?" He might answer, "I have seen you many a time in God's house. We have sung together, prayed together, and worshiped together in the same sanctuary, but it is all over now. I shall never see you anymore!" "What, never; minister? Never hear your voice again?" "No, never, unless you are in Christ now, farewell forever!" O poor soul, what a sorrowful thing to shake hands forever, to bid good-bye forever—one to descend to endless flames and the other to mount to realms of everlasting bliss! We may, indeed, sorrow for them if we have no hope of ever meeting them again.

But we should not grieve so much about not meeting them again if we knew that they were happy, even though we should never see them. But, then, for those who die without Christ, we sorrow because we have no hope that they have any happiness. Or even if they were now in misery, and we might cherish the thought that they would one day escape, we should not then sorrow for them as those that have no hope. But, alas! we recollect that our lost friends are lost forever. We recollect that there is no shadow of a hope for them. When the iron gate of hell is once closed upon them, it shall never be unbarred again to give them free exit. When once shut up within those walls of sweltering flame that girdle the fiery gulf, there is no possibility of flight. We recollect that they have "forever" stamped upon their chains, "forever" carved in deep lines of despair upon their hearts. It is the hell of hell that everything there lasts forever. Here, time wears away our griefs and blunts the keen edge of sorrow. But there, time never mitigates the woe. Here, the sympathy of loving kindred, in the midst of sickness or suffering, can alleviate our pain. But there, the mutual upbraidings and reproaches of fellow sinners give fresh stings to torment too dreadful to be endured. Here, too, when nature's last palliative shall fail, to die may be a happy release. A man can count the weary hours until death shall give him rest. But, oh! remember, there is no death in hell. Death, which is a monster on earth, would be an angel in hell. But the terrible reality is this, "Their worm dieth not, and the fire is not quenched" (Mark 9:44, 46, 48).

Must we go one step further? It is terrible work to deliver these warnings, but it would be more terrible still to hide any truth, however bitter. When we have uttered a pitiful lament for heathen nations, and when we have spoken with deeper emotion of the profane, the profligate, and the despisers of God, we have not done. These have not the semblance of peace in their own breasts. But alas! alas! there are many who die in the delusion of a false peace. What avails it that they uttered pious sentiments with their lips if their hearts were not changed? What though they received "the bread and wine" in nature's extremity? Will the sacramental opiate serve them instead of the inward witness of reconciliation to God? Oh, hear this, you that are at ease; listen, all you whose religion stands in outward forms: "Like sheep they are laid in the grave; death shall feed on them; and the upright shall have dominion over them in the morning" (Ps. 49:14). I confess to you that the metaphor which charms me in the one case appalls me in the other, so great is the distinction among the sleepers. Look at the man who has sought to be justified by the works of the law or in some way perverted the gospel of Christ. With a fatal lull of conscience he nestles down securely, "as when an hungry man dreameth, and, behold, he eateth; but he awaketh, and his soul is empty: or as when a thirsty man dreameth, and, behold, he drinketh; but he awaketh, and, behold, he is faint, and his soul hath appetite" (Isa. 29:8). He sleeps the deep sleep of death, prepared, as he supposes, to meet the Judge. When he awakes, the spell shall be dissolved. The terrible sentence, "Depart," awaits him. O beloved, I tremble to think that a man may go up with jaunty step to the threshold of heaven only to be cast down to the nethermost pit! As you stand among the graves of your departed friends, I beseech you to examine yourselves. Only as you can say, "To me to live is Christ," have you a right to add, "and to die is gain" (Phil. 1:21).

But now there is the case of the Christian. Is it not matter for consolation and holy joy with some of us, that, concerning beloved friends of ours who now sleep quietly in their graves, we have not to sorrow as those who have no hope? The death of the saints is precious in the sight of the Lord. On their account we have cause rather to rejoice than to weep. And why? Because we hope that they are safely housed in heaven. Yea, more, we have the firm persuasion that already their redeemed spirits have flown up to the eternal throne. We do believe that they are at this moment joining in the hallelujahs of paradise, feasting on the fruits of the tree of life, and walking by the side of the river, the streams whereof make glad the heavenly city of our God. We know they are supremely blest. We think of them as glorified spirits above, who are "forever with the Lord."

We have that hope. Then we have another hope concerning them—we hope that, though we have buried them, they shall rise again. In the verse following our text it is written, "Them also which sleep in Jesus will God bring with him" (1 Thess. 4:14). We rejoice that not only do "they . . . rest from their labours; and their works do follow them" (Rev. 14:13); but that, after they have rested a little while, their bodies shall rise again. We know that their Redeemer lives. We are certain that He will, at the latter day, stand upon the earth and that they shall stand on the earth with Him. We rejoice that the dead in Christ shall rise first and that they shall come on that day when, with clouds descending, "he shall come to be glorified in his saints, and to be admired in all them that believe" (2 Thess. 1:10). We look for a day when buried bodies shall be living frames once more. We expect that glazed eyes shall again be radiant with light. We believe that dumb lips shall yet sing, that deaf ears shall yet hear, and that lame feet shall yet leap like the hart.

We are looking for the time when we shall meet the saints in their very bodies and shall know them, too. It is our hope that they shall rise again, and that we shall meet them and shall know them. I trust you all firmly believe that you will recognize your friends in heaven. I consider the doctrine of the nonrecognition of our friends in heaven a marvelously absurd one. I cannot conceive how there can be any communion of saints in heaven unless there be mutual recognition. We could not hold communion with unknown beings. If we knew not who they were, how should we be able to join their company? Moreover, we are told that we shall "sit down with Abraham, and Isaac, and Jacob" (Matt. 8:11). I suppose we shall know those blessed patriarchs when we sit down with them. If we know them, there is but one step to the supposition that we shall know all the general assembly. Moreover, there will be but very little difficulty in discovering them because every seed has its own body. By which we are taught that every body being different from any other body when sown will, when it rises in a spiritual fashion, be in like manner different from any other. Although the spiritual body may have none of the lineaments upon its face like we have and no marks as we have, because it will be far more glorious and splendid, yet it will have so much identity that we, being instructed, shall be able to say of it, "This is the body that sprang from such a seed," just as we recognize the different kinds of corn or flowers that spring from the different kinds of seed that are sown. Take away recognition, and you have taken away, I think, one of the joys of heaven. There seems to me a great deal of heaven's sweetness in the little verse (to quote another of the children's hymns),

> Teachers, too, shall meet above,
> And our pastors whom we love
> Shall meet to part no more.

A Gentle Exhortation

The exhortation here is delicately hinted at, that the sorrow of bereaved Christians for their Christian friends ought not to be at all like the sorrow of unconverted persons for their ungodly relatives. We are not forbidden to sorrow: "Jesus wept" (John 11:35). The gospel does not teach us to be Stoics. We ought to weep, for it was intended that the rod should be felt, otherwise we could not "hear ye the rod, and who hath appointed it" (Mic. 6:9). If we did not feel the stroke when our friends were taken away, we should prove ourselves worse than heathen men and publicans. God's grace does not take away our sensibilities, it only refines them, and in some degree restrains the violence of their expression. Still, there ought to be some difference between the sorrow of the righteous and the sorrow of the wicked.

First, *there should be a difference in its vehemence.* It may be natural to the unbridled passions of an ungodly man who has lost his wife to tear his hair, to throw himself upon the bed, to clutch the body, to declare it shall not be buried, to rave through the house cursing God and saying all manner of hard things of his dispensations. But that would not do for a Christian. He must not murmur. A Christian man may stand and weep. He may kiss the dear cold hand for the last time and rain showers of tears on the lifeless body while "pity swells the tide of love"; but God and his religion demand that he should say, after doing this, "The LORD gave, and the LORD hath taken away; blessed be the name of the LORD" (Job 1:21). He may weep—he ought to; he may sorrow—he ought to; he may wear the habiliments of mourning—God forbid that we should ever believe in any religion that should proscribe our showing some outward signs of sorrow for our friends!—yet we may not, and we must not, weep as others weep. We must not always carry the red and tearful eye. We must not always take with us the face that is downcast and distressed. If we do, the world will say of us that our conduct belies our profession, and our feelings are at variance with our faith.

Again, there is another thing we must never allow to enter into our grief—*the least degree of repining.* A wicked man, when he sorrows for those who are gone without hope, not infrequently murmurs against God. But it is far otherwise with the Christian. He meekly bows his head and says, "Thy will, O God, be done." The Christian must still acknowledge the same gracious hand of God, whether it be stretched forth to give or to take away. The language of his faith is, "Though he slay me, yet will I trust in him" (Job 13:15); or "though He should take all away, yet will I not repine." I do not say that all Christian persons are able to maintain such a cheerful submission of spirit. I only say that they ought, and that such is the tendency of the Christian religion. If they had more of the Spirit of God within their hearts, that would be their habitual disposition. We may sorrow, beloved, but not with repining. There must be resignation mixed with the regret. There must be the yielding up, even with grateful acquiescence, that which God asks for, seeing we believe that He does but take what is His own.

And now, there is just one further observation. I do believe that, *when the Christian sorrows, he ought to be as glad as he is sorrowful.* Put your sadness in one scale and your gladness in the other scale, then see if the reasons for praise be not as weighty as the reasons for grief. Then you will say, "She is gone; there is a tear for her. She is in heaven; there is a smile for her. Her body is with the worms; weep, eyes. Her soul is with Jesus; shout, lips, aye, shout for joy. The cold sod has covered her, she is gone from my sight, she sleeps in the sad, sad grave; bring me the habiliments of mourning. No, she is before the throne of God and the Lamb, blest for aye. Lend me a harp and let me thank my God she has joined the white-robed host on yonder blessed plains. O hearse and funeral, O shroud and garments of woe, you are most fitting for her! I have lost her, and she herself, with many a pang and struggle, has passed through the valley of the shallow of death. But O joyous face! O songs of gladness! O shouts of rapture! You are equally becoming! For when she passed through the valley of the shadow of death, she feared no evil, for Your rod and Your staff did comfort her. Now, beyond the reach of death's alarms, she does bathe her soul in seas of bliss. She is with her Lord."

It is well to have a little singing as well as weeping at a funeral. It well becomes the burial of the saints. Angels never weep when saints die—they sing. You never heard a saint say when he was dying, "There are angels in the room; hark! you can hear them sobbing because I am dying." No; but we have often heard a saint say, "There are angels in the room, and I can hear them singing." That is because angels are wiser than we are. We judge by the sight of our eyes and the hearing of our ears. But angels judge after another fashion. They "see and hear and know" the joys of the blest, and, therefore, they have no tears. But they have songs for them, and they sing loudly when the Christian is carried home like a shock of corn fully ripe.

And now, beloved, we shall soon all of us die. In a few more years, I shall have a gravestone above my grave. Some of you, I hope, will say, "There lies our minister, who once gathered us together in the house of God and led us to the mercy seat and joined in our song. There lies one who was often despised and rejected of men, but whom God did nevertheless bless to the salvation of our souls, and sealed his testimony in our hearts and consciences by the operation of the Holy Spirit." Perhaps some of you will visit my tomb and will bring a few flowers to scatter on it, in glad and grateful remembrance of the happy hours we spent together. It is quite as probable that your tombs will be built as soon as mine. Ah, dear friends! should we have to write on your tombstones, "She sleeps in Jesus," "He rests in the bosom of his Master," or should we have to speak the honest truth, "He has gone to his own place"? Which shall it be? Ask yourselves, each one of you, where will your soul be? Shall it mount up there,

> Where our best friends, our kindred, dwell,
>   Where God our Savior reigns;

or,

> Shall devils plunge you down to hell,
>   In infinite despair?

You can ascertain which it will be. You can tell it by this: Do you believe on the Lord Jesus Christ? Do you love the Lord Jesus? Do you stand on Christ, the solid rock? Have you built your hope of heaven alone on Him? Have you, as a guilty sinner, cast yourself at His mercy seat, looking to His blood and righteousness, to be saved by them, and by them alone? If so, fear not to die. You shall be safe whenever the summons comes to you. But if not, tremble, tremble! you may die tomorrow—you must die one day. It will be a sad thing so to die as to be lost beyond recovery. May God Almighty grant that we may be all saved at last, for Jesus' sake! Amen.

The Village Tragedy

Clovis Gillham Chappell (1882–1972) was one of American Methodism's best-known and most effective preachers. He pastored churches in Washington, D.C.; Dallas and Houston, Texas; Memphis, Tennessee; and Birmingham, Alabama; and his pulpit ministry drew great crowds. He was especially known for his biographical sermons that made biblical figures live and speak to our modern day. He published about thirty volumes of sermons.

This message was taken from *The Village Tragedy*, published in New York in 1975 by Abingdon Press.

2

The Village Tragedy

Then said Jesus unto them plainly, Lazarus is dead. (John 11:14)

FOR MOST OF US that is the last word. There is nothing else to be said. The worst possible has already happened. The grimmest of all grim tragedies has already been enacted. Lazarus is dead—the nurse may now go home. The physician, faithful to the last, may return to his office. Medicines, poultices, ministering hands are no longer needed. Disease has done its grim work—Lazarus is dead.

What an old tragedy this is, how commonplace. When the hearse passed you on the street yesterday you hardly turned your head. It is soon forgotten. It is so usual. It is so ordinary. And yet how new is this tragedy. How it comes to you with a freshness of pain and heartache and despair as if you were the first and only one that had ever looked into the glazed eyes of somebody you loved.

Remember it was just that new to Martha and Mary. There had not been a happier home in the little village of Bethany than theirs. They had that which above all else makes for happiness—they had love one for the other. Lazarus and Martha and Mary loved each other. Then they had love for Jesus. And that forms a sure basis for a happy home. There is no other foundation like it.

But Lazarus is dead. He who was the head of the house, he who was their protector—Lazarus, the loved brother, is gone out beyond the hearing of their voices and beyond the reach of their hands. And their home from being the happiest of the village is now the saddest and the gloomiest and the darkest and the most hopeless. The light has gone out. The sun has set. Home can never be again what it was in the good old days. How they had loved and rejoiced in this little village home. How they had made others love and rejoice in it. How openhanded they were in their hospitality. Their home was the preacher's home. I think there was scarcely a home in the world where Jesus found so warm a welcome. I think there was no other place where He found more responsive and understanding hearts. But all has changed now. Nothing can ever be the same again—Lazarus is dead.

Just how this fatal sickness slipped upon Lazarus we do not know. We are not told how intense was his suffering. We are not told how long he lingered. But be assured of this, that from the day he was taken sick he was nursed with the tenderest care and solicitude. And many a time did the sisters say to each other, "If Jesus would only come." And there was a great dread lest death should put his ghastly foot across the doorsill before their favored Guest should come again.

At last they were unable to endure the suspense and anxiety longer. They sent a messenger to Jesus. And while this messenger carried only the statement of a fact, that statement had in it unuttered prayers sweet with faith and wet with tears. "He whom thou lovest is sick" (John 11:3). That was the message. That was all they said. That was all they felt there was any need to say. They did not tell Jesus what to do. They did not bid Him hurry to the bedside of His friend. They told Him the simple, sorrowful fact, "He whom thou lovest is sick."

Then followed those testing days of waiting. How many times they went to look out the window no one will ever know. How many times one of them stole through the door and down beyond the bend of the road we can only guess. But be assured of this fact, they watched and waited and hoped. But death came before He came. Then they hoped He would be there for the funeral. But they went to the grave alone and came home alone. And even yet Jesus had not come.

Now why was this tragedy allowed to take place? Why must Lazarus suffer? Why must death lay hold of him? Why must his sisters be called upon to pass through this Gethsemane? I am sure that these questions perplexed these two sisters long ago, just as they sometimes perplex ourselves and wring our own hearts.

This tragedy did not take place because of the ignorance of Jesus. They were sure of that. Fearing that He might not know, they sent a messenger to tell Him. They had to realize that Jesus knew all about it. He knew the pain of Lazarus. He knew their own anguish and bitter aching of heart. And I like to think just as He knew all about Lazarus and Martha and Mary as they went through their great trial, so He knows all about you and me. Jesus knows.

So it was not ignorance on the part of Christ that allowed this tragedy to take place. Neither was it His powerlessness. Martha and Mary were convinced of that. They felt that He could have prevented it if He had only been there. They were somehow confident that if He had stood in the door, even mighty death could never have slipped in past Him. They were sure that His presence would have been enough. They were confident that His might was sufficient even for the defeating of the grim purpose of death.

Neither is the death of Lazarus a mark of the lack of love on the part of Jesus. That fact is made blessedly plain to us. "He whom thou lovest is sick," said the message. And many folks are sick whom Jesus loves. Do not understand me to deny for a moment the power of Jesus to heal the sick. He has that power. But mark me, He does not exercise it in every case. Many a loved saint of God is sick and will continue sick until they reach that blessed country where the winsome Physician "waits with eternal healing in His fingers."

The fact that Lazarus sickened and suffered and died was then not a mark of the lack of love on the part of Jesus. It was rather a mark of the opposite. Will you notice this strange sentence: "Now Jesus loved Martha, and her sister, and Lazarus. When he had heard therefore that he was sick, he abode two days still in the same place where he was" (John 11:5).

The Love of Jesus

First we read that He loved these three. He did not love them as a family simply. He loved them as individuals. Christ's love, like our own, is a personal and individual something. He does not love men in the mass. He does not save men in the mass. He loves and seeks and saves the individual. My father and mother had quite a large family of children. But they did not love us as a group simply. They called us each by name and loved us each individually. I love to think of their love for all their children. I like to think also of their love for me. I love to think of Christ's love for a world, but I like to say with Paul, "[He] loved me, and gave himself for me" (Gal. 2:20).

Jesus then loved these three individually, personally. Therefore He stayed away from them in the hour of their dire need. He loved them; therefore He delayed until Lazarus died and until there was the setting of a great hope in the lives of the two sisters that was like the setting of the sun. What a strange "therefore" this is! He loved them; therefore He hastened to go to their assistance—that is what we would have expected. He loved them; therefore as soon as He found they were in trouble He made haste to help. But instead we read, "He loved them; therefore He stayed away. He loved them; therefore He allowed disease to have its way with Lazarus and death to enter in unafraid."

This is a lesson we need to learn again and again, that love sometimes sees best to let us suffer. So often we feel that ease and exemption from pain, success and prosperity—that these only are marks of God's love and of God's favor. It is an old idea that has haunted the thought of the church through the centuries. The old time Sunday school story used to have a good boy and a bad boy. And the bad boy was always getting the worst of it and the good boy was always getting the pie. But it is wrong and altogether wrong. Many wicked men prosper. Many good men go to the wall and fail. But this does not mean that God loves the one and does not love the other.

God loved Martha, her sister, and Lazarus; therefore He will let Lazarus die. God loves you, therefore He brought to you that great disappointment. God loves you, therefore He put the hand of affliction upon you. God loves you, therefore you were called to kneel by the coffin of your dearest and best. God loved Paul, therefore He allowed him to be afflicted with a thorn in the flesh. And it was on that grim and forbidding thorn that Paul found in after years growing the rarest and sweetest flowers.

Why then was this tragedy allowed to take place? It was because Christ loved these people. It was because He loves us. And loving them and loving us, He wanted to give us a new and deeper and more wonderful knowledge of Himself. "I am glad," He said to His disciples, "for your sakes that I was not there, to the intent ye may believe" (John 11:15) He was glad because He knew that it is only through pain that life's greatest lessons are learned. He knew that the choicest souls all through the centuries are the souls that have suffered.

Do you remember Gwen in "The Sky Pilot," that charming little story by Ralph Connor? She was a wild, willful thing, loving above all else the great out-of-doors, the plains and the deep, cool canyons. A wonderful rider she was, and her pony brought this loved world within her daily enjoyment. But it came to pass that her pony fell with her. She was caught under him and so badly crippled that she could never ride again. And now up in the little cabin at the head of the canyon she was lying day after day, bitter, raving, rebellious, fretting her life away.

One day the Sky Pilot came to see her. And he was brave enough to tell her the story of the canyons. He told her how that the Master of the prairie one day walked out over the plains, and though He found many lovely flowers, He missed the ones that He loved best. He then sent the birds and the winds to plant these flowers. But they had no sooner sprung up than they withered away. At last in seeming anger the Master sent a thunderbolt and cleft the prairie to the heart. For a long time it groaned with the pain of its black wound. Then the birds and the winds again scattered the seeds of the flowers that the Master loved best. And the fairest flowers to be found in all the land were those that grew in the canyon, the once ugly wound. And a cool sweet place it was with all its shades and songs and silences.

And now Gwen's eyes were opened and her heart as well. She was no longer rebellious. She became strangely sweet and strangely patient and tender, for into her wounded life the King had come. And He planted in her soul garden the flowers that

He loves the best. There were love, joy, peace, long-suffering, gentleness, and goodness. And while these flowers bloom in every heart in which the King is gardener, yet it does seem that they grow in their richest profusion in the garden of those hearts that have been wounded and broken.

What did Jesus teach these tearful women years ago? And what does He teach us through their great sorrow? First, He teaches us that the fact that we suffer, that the fact that our hearts ache and break sometimes—does not necessarily mean that He Himself is absent. Martha and Mary felt that if Jesus had only been there this could never have happened. But in reality He was there. Nothing had taken place without His knowledge. Nothing had taken place without His will. All the while that death was doing its grim work, Jesus was there, "closer than breathing and nearer than hands and feet."

I know that there is suffering that comes because of the absence of Jesus. "Lord, if thou hadst been here, my brother had not died [morally]" (John 11:21, 32)—many a man can say that who has been unfaithful to his brother. "Lord, if You had been here my son had not died morally"—many a father can say that over whose ragged and unfaithful life his boy has stumbled out into a life of death in trespasses and in sin. If Christ had been in your home your children would not be the heartache that they are today. If Christ had been in your home it would not be the wreck it is today. How many men and women there are who are separated and whose children are robbed of the privileges of a complete home because of sin. Jesus was not there—that is the reason you let lust put its grim handcuffs upon you. Jesus was not there—that is the reason you made a hell out of your humble little home. Yes, many a broken heart may say, "If You had been here this tragedy would never have taken place." But this was not the case with Martha and Mary. They learned, and we learn, that Jesus may be very near to us even though we suffer, even though our hearts ache and bleed and break.

The Sympathy of Jesus

They learned, in the second place, the wonderful lesson of the sympathy of Jesus. This chapter holds in its hands one of the sweetest sentences ever penned, "Jesus wept" (John 11:35).

How human He was, how tender, how sympathetic. The thorn crown, the agonies of the cross could not make Him weep, but He wept at the sorrows of these who loved Him.

What a blessed something is sympathy. There is enough in a look, in a handshake, in a smile sometimes to keep our hopes from dying and our hearts from breaking. How much all of us owe to the sympathy that has been given us along the way. But the most real thing in the world is the sympathy of Jesus. In all our afflictions He is afflicted. And there is never a darkened home but that Jesus is there. And there is never a broken heart and never an open grave but that Christ is there. In patience He waits to be recognized. He longs to extend His sympathy. He yearns to "kiss our tears into jewels" and change our night into marvelous day.

The Assurance of the After Life

Then, last of all, there came to these, as there comes to ourselves today, a new and satisfying assurance of the reality of the after life. Christ lets us know here, first of all, that the after life is a present fact. You remember how He said to Martha, "Thy brother shall rise again" (John 11:23). But she had heard that encouragement again and again from the Jews until she had grown tired. And there is disappointment that amounts almost to impatience in her answer, "I know that he shall rise again in the resurrection at the last day" (v. 24). But what she means to say is, "But Master, that is so far off. That is so mysterious, so uncertain, so dim and distant in the haze of the eternities."

Will you note the answer that Christ makes: "I am the resurrection, and the life" (v. 25). Christ is saying, "I am not distant. I am not future. I am here. I am an eternal, present fact." So life, eternal life, is an abidingly present reality. "To be absent from the body," as Paul tells us, "[is] to be present with the Lord" (2 Cor. 5:8). The dead live now, not "shall live by and by." Our God is the God of Abraham, Isaac, and Jacob. Therefore Abraham and Isaac and Jacob still live. For God, Christ tells us, is not the God of the dead, but of the living.

Then Christ not only teaches us that the after life is a present fact, but He teaches us also the survival of individuality in that after life. When He stands by the grave to raise Lazarus from the dead, He does not call him by some new name, He called him by the name by which He had known him in this life. And those that have passed into that larger life "still answer to their old names." Elijah is still Elijah as he comes on the Mount of Transfiguration, though he has been dead for centuries. And Moses is still Moses. And do not doubt that those that you love still answer to their old names in God's house.

There is a story of how a beautiful Saracen girl fell in love with one of the Crusaders who had gone into Palestine to deliver the Holy Sepulcher. He was unable to take her back to England with him, so in after days she made the long journey alone. At last she reached London. She knew not one word of English. She only knew the name of the man she loved, and she went through London's streets calling that name. And she did not call in vain. The glad moment came when her knight answered and took her to his heart. And so you and I one day shall call familiar names in that other "city . . . whose builder and maker is God" (Heb. 11:10), and familiar faces shall answer to those old names.

And Jesus not only teaches the present tense of this that we call the afterlife; He not only teaches the survival of personality— He teaches also the survival of love. He teaches the survival of the sweet old relationships that have made life the blessed and fascinating experience that it is in the here and now. When He speaks of Lazarus, as another has pointed out, He says, "Our friend Lazarus" (John 11:11). Yes, on the other side of the river Lazarus is still a friend to Jesus, and Jesus is still a friend to Lazarus. Death can kill a body but it cannot kill love. When He speaks to Martha He says, "Thy brother." Lazarus had slipped out of the old home. Lazarus's body was decaying in the tomb, but Lazarus was not dead. He was still living. He was still the brother of Martha and of Mary. They were still his sisters. And that sweet relationship was beyond the reach of the destroying hand of death.

How many hungry hearts have asked this question: "Shall we know each other there?" On the authority of my Lord I feel justified in saying there is not the slightest doubt of it. There is certainly not in my own mind. And you are justified in saying, "My baby," not simply of the one that is still in your home, but also of that one who has toddled out of your home into that other home not made with hands. You have a right still to speak of those who have gone on before as "My husband" and "My wife" and "My friend" and "My boy." These that have died in the knowledge of Jesus are still ours. And one day God will give them back to us with our old loves cleansed and purified in the Land of Eternal Gladness.

Heart, I wonder today if this faith is your faith. I wonder if this Christ who is present no less in our sorrows than in our joys, I wonder if this Christ who sympathizes, this mighty Christ who flings open the door of the life eternal to us—is your Christ. If He is, I am sure that you consider no price too great to have paid to have come so to know Him. You may have come to this glad knowledge through heartache, as did these people years ago. But if you did, I am sure that you have come to recognize, as did Martha and Mary and Lazarus, that their darkest day was also their brightest and sweetest and best. Our Lord does not deal with all of us alike, but His purpose for all is this same high and holy purpose, that we may come to know Him. This is the end He has in view in all our laughter and all our tears. If He can only get us to lay hold on His hand He knows that that will mean life eternal here and life eternal yonder in His presence, with those "that we have loved long since and lost a while."

A Prisoner's Dying Thoughts

Alexander Maclaren (1826–1910) was one of Great Britain's most famous preachers. While pastoring the Union Chapel, Manchester (1858–1903), he became known as "the prince of expository preachers." Rarely active in denominational or civic affairs, Maclaren invested his time in studying the Word in the original languages and in sharing its truths with others in sermons that are still models of effective expository preaching. He published a number of books of sermons and climaxed his ministry by publishing his monumental *Expositions of Holy Scripture*.

This message was taken from *The Secret of Power*, published by Funk and Wagnalls in 1902.

ALEXANDER MACLAREN

3

A Prisoner's Dying Thoughts

> I am now ready to be offered, and the time of my departure is at hand. I have fought a good fight, I have finished my course, I have kept the faith: henceforth there is laid up for me a crown of righteousness. (2 Timothy 4:6–8)

PAUL'S LONG DAY'S WORK is nearly done. He is a prisoner in Rome, all but forsaken by his friends, in hourly expectation of another summons before Nero. To appear before him was, he says, like putting his head into "the mouth of the lion" (2 Tim. 4:17). His horizon was darkened by sad anticipations of decaying faith and growing corruption in the church. What a road he had traveled since that day when, on the way to Damascus, he saw the living Christ and heard the words of His mouth!

It had been but a failure of a life, if judged by ordinary standards. He had suffered the loss of all things, had thrown away position and prospects, had exposed himself to sorrows and toils, had been all his days a poor man and solitary, had been hunted, despised, laughed at by Jew and Gentile, and worried and badgered even by so-called brethren. Loved the less, the more he loved. And now the end is near. A prison and the headsman's sword are the world's wages to its best teacher. When Nero is on the throne, the only possible place for Paul is the dungeon opening on to the scaffold. Better to be the martyr than the Caesar!

These familiar words of our text bring before us a very sweet and wonderful picture of the prisoner, so near his end. How beautifully they show his calm waiting for the last hour and the bright forms that lightened for him the darkness of his cell! Many since have gone to their rest with their hearts stayed on the same thoughts, though their lips could not speak them to our listening ears. Let us be thankful for them, and pray that for ourselves, when we come to that hour, the same quiet heroism and the same sober hope mounting to calm certainty may be ours.

These words refer to the past, the present, the future. "I have fought—the time of my departure is come—henceforth there is laid up."

The Quiet Courage That Looks Death Full in the Face Without a Tremor

The language implies that Paul knows his death hour is all but here. As the Revised Version more accurately gives it, "I am already being offered"—the process is begun, his sufferings at the moment are, as it were, the initial steps of his sacrifice—"and the time of my departure is *come*." The tone in which he tells Timothy this is very noticeable. There is no sign of excitement, no tremor of emotion, no affectation of stoicism in the simple sentences. He is not playing up to a part, nor pretending to be anything which he is not. If ever language sounded perfectly simple and genuine, this does.

And the occasion of the whole section is as remarkable as the tone. He is led to speak about himself at all, only in order to enforce his exhortation to Timothy to put his shoulder to the wheel and do his work for Christ with all his might. All he wishes to say is simply, Do your work with all your might, for I am going off the field. But having begun on that line of thought, he is carried on to say more than was needed for his immediate purpose, and thus inartificially to let us see what was filling his mind.

And the subject into which he subsides after these lofty thoughts is as remarkable as either tone or occasion. Minute directions about such small matters as books and parchments, and perhaps a warm cloak for winter, and homely details about the movements of the little group of his friends immediately follow. All this shows with what a perfectly unforced courage Paul fronted his fate and looked death in the eyes. The anticipation did not dull his interest in God's work in the world, as witness the warnings and exhortations of the context. It did not withdraw his sympathies from his companions. It did not hinder him from pursuing his studies and pursuits, nor from providing for small matters of daily convenience. If ever a man was free from any taint of fanaticism or morbid enthusiasm, it was this man waiting so calmly in his prison for his death.

There is great beauty and force in the expressions which he uses for death here. He will not soil his lips with its ugly name, but calls it an offering and a departure. There is a widespread unwillingness to say the word "Death." It falls on men's hearts like clods on a coffin—so all people and languages have adopted euphemisms for it, fair names which wrap silk around his dart and somewhat hide his face. But there are two opposite reasons for their use—terror and confidence. Some men dare not speak of death because they dread it so much, and try to put some kind of shield between themselves and the very thought of it by calling it something less dreadful to them than itself. Some men, on the other hand, are familiar with the thought, and though it is solemn, it is not altogether repellent to them. Gazing on death with the thoughts and feelings that Jesus Christ has given them concerning it, they see it in new aspects, which take away much of its blackness. And so they do not feel inclined to use the ugly old name, but had rather call it by some which reflect the gentler aspect that it now wears to them. So "sleep" and "rest" and the like are the names that have almost driven the other out of the New Testament—witness of the fact that in inmost reality Jesus Christ "hath abolished death" (2 Tim. 1:10), however the physical portion of it may still remain master of our bodies.

But looking for a moment at the specific metaphors used here, we have first, that of an *offering*, or more particularly of a drink offering, or *libation*, "I am already being poured out." No doubt the special reason for the selection of this figure here is Paul's anticipation of a violent death. The shedding of his blood was to be an offering poured out like some costly wine upon the altar, but the power of the figure reaches far beyond that special application of it. We may all make our deaths a sacrifice, an offering to God, for we may yield up our will to God's will, and so turn that last struggle into an act of worship and self surrender. When we recognize His hand, when we submit our wills to His purposes, when "we live unto the Lord"—if we live—and "die unto the Lord" (Rom. 14:8)—if we die—then death will lose all its terror and most of its pain and will become for us what it was to Paul, a true offering up of self in thankful worship. No, we may even say, that so we shall in a certain subordinate sense be "made conformable unto his death" (Phil. 3:10) who committed His spirit into His Father's hands and laid down His life, of His own will. The essential character and far-reaching effects of this sacrifice we cannot imitate, but we can so yield up our wills to God and leave life so willingly and trustfully as that death shall make our sacrifice complete.

Another more familiar and equally striking figure is next used when Paul speaks of the time of his "departure." The thought is found in most tongues. Death is a going away, or, as Peter calls it (with a glance, possibly, at the special meaning of the word in the Old Testament, as well as its use in the solemn statement of the theme of converse on the Mountain of Transfiguration), an Exodus. But the well-worn image receives new depth and sharpness of outline in Christianity. To those who have learned the meaning of Christ's resurrection, and feed their souls on the hopes that it warrants, death is merely a change of place or state, an accident affecting locality, and little more. We have had plenty of changes before. Life has been one long series of departures. This is different from the others mainly in that it is the last, and that to go away from this visible and fleeting show, where we wander aliens among things that have no true kindred with us, is to go home, where there will be no more pulling up the tent-pegs, and toiling across the deserts in monotonous change. How strong is the conviction, spoken in that name for death, that the essential life lasts on quite unaltered through it all! How slight the else formidable thing is made. We may change climates, and for the stormy bleakness of life may have the long still days of heaven, but we do not change ourselves. We lose nothing worth keeping when we leave behind the body, as a dress not fitted for home, where we are going. We but travel one more stage, though it be the last, and part of it be in pitch darkness. Some pass over it as in a fiery chariot, like Paul and many a martyr. Some have to toil through it with slow steps and bleeding feet and fainting heart. But all may have a Brother with them, and holding His hand may find that the journey is not so hard as they feared, and the home from which they shall remove no more, better than they hoped when they hoped the most.

The Peaceful Look Backward

There is something very noteworthy in the threefold aspect under which his past life presents itself to the apostle, who is so soon to leave it. He thinks of it as a contest, as a race, as a stewardship. The first suggests the tension of a long struggle with opposing wrestlers who have tried to throw him, but in vain. The world, both of men and things, has had to be grappled with and mastered. His own sinful nature and especially his animal nature has had to be kept under by sheer force, and every moment has been resistance to subtle omnipresent forces that have sought to thwart his aspirations and hamper his performances. His successes have had to be fought for, and everything that he has done has been done after a struggle. So is it with all noble life; so will it be to the end.

He thinks of life as a race. That speaks of continuous advance in one direction and, more emphatically still, of effort that sets the lungs panting and strains every muscle to the utmost. He thinks of it as a stewardship. He has kept the faith (whether by that word we are to understand the body of truth believed or the act of believing) as a sacred deposit committed to him, of which he has been a good steward, and which he is now ready to return to his Lord. There is much in these letters to Timothy about keeping treasures entrusted to one's care. Timothy is bid to keep "that good thing which was committed unto thee" (2 Tim. 1:14), as Paul here declares that he has done. Nor is such guarding of a precious deposit confined to us stewards on earth, but the apostle is sure that his loving Lord, to whom he has entrusted himself, will with like tenderness and carefulness "keep that which [he has] committed unto him against that day" (v. 12). The confidence in that faithful Keeper made it possible for Paul to be faithful to his trust, and as a steward who was bound by all ties to his Lord, to guard His possessions and administer His affairs. Life was full of voices urging him to give up the faith. Bribes and threats, and his own sense-bound nature, and the constant whispers of the world had tempted him all along the road to fling it away as a worthless thing, but he had kept it safe. Now, nearing the end and the account, he can put his hand on the secret place near his heart where it lies, and feel that it is there, ready to be restored to his Lord, with the thankful confession, "Thy pound hath gained ten pounds" (Luke 19:16).

So life looks to this man in his retrospect as mainly a field for struggle, effort, and fidelity. This world is not to be for us an enchanted garden of delights, any more than it should appear a dreary desert of disappointment and woe. But it should be to us mainly a palaestra, or gymnasium and exercising ground. You cannot expect many flowers or much grass in the place where men wrestle and run. We need not much mind though it be bare, if we can only stand firm on the hard earth, nor lament that there are so few delights to stay our eyes from the goal. We are here for serious work. Let us not be too eager for pleasures that may hinder our efforts and weaken our vigor, but be content to lap up a hasty draught from the brooks by the way, and then on again to the fight.

Such a view of life makes it radiant and fair while it lasts, and makes the heart calm when the hour comes to leave it all behind. So thinking of the past, there may be a sense of not unwelcome lightening from a load of responsibility when we have gotten all the stress and strain of the conflict behind us, and have, at any rate, not been altogether beaten. We may feel like a captain who has brought his ship safe across the Atlantic through foul weather and past many an iceberg, and gives a great sigh of relief as he hands over the charge to the pilot, who will take her across the harbor bar and bring her to her anchorage in the landlocked bay where no tempests rave anymore forever.

Prosaic theologians have sometimes wondered at the estimate which Paul here makes of his past services and faithfulness, but the wonder is surely unnecessary. It is very striking to notice the difference between his judgment of himself while he was still in the thick of the conflict, and now when he is nearing the end. Then, one main hope which animated all his toils and nerved him for the sacrifice of life itself was "that I might finish my course with joy." Now, in the quiet of his dungeon, that hope is fulfilled and triumphant thoughts, like shining angels, keep him company in his solitude. Then he struggles and wrestles, touched by the haunting fear lest after that he has preached to others he himself should be rejected. Now the dread has passed and a meek hope stands by his side.

What is this change of feeling but an instance of what, thank God, we so often see, that at the end the heart which has been bowed with fears and self-depreciation is filled with peace? They who tremble most during the conflict are most likely to look back with solid satisfaction, while they who never knew a fear all along the course will often have them surging in upon their souls too late, and will see the past in a new lurid light, when they are powerless to change it. Blessed is the man who thus fears always. At the end he will have hope. The past struggles are joyful in memory, as the mountain ranges, which were all black rock and white snow while we toiled up their inhospitable steeps, lie purple in the mellowing distance and burn like fire as the sunset strikes their peaks. Many a wild winter's day has a fair cloudless close, and lingering opal hues diffused through all the quiet sky. "At eventide it shall be light." Though we go all our lives mourning and timid, there may yet be granted us before the end some vision of the true significance of these lives, and some humble hope that they have not been wholly in vain.

Such an estimate has nothing in common with self-complacency. It coexists with a profound consciousness of many a sin, many a defeat, and much unfaithfulness. It belongs only to a man who, conscious of these, is "looking for the mercy of our Lord Jesus Christ unto eternal life" (Jude 21), and is the direct result, not the antagonist, of lowly self-abasement and contrite faith in Him by whom alone our stained selves and poor broken services can ever be acceptable. Let us learn too that the only life that bears being looked back upon is a life of Christian devotion and effort.

It shows fairer when seen in the strange cross lights that come when we stand on the boundary of two worlds, with the white radiance of eternity beginning to master the vulgar oil lamps of earth, than when seen by these alone. All others have their shabbiness and their selfishness disclosed then. I remember once seeing a mob of revelers streaming out from a masked ball in a London theater in the early morning sunlight, draggled and heavy-eyed, the rouge showing on the cheeks, and the shabby tawdriness of the foolish costumes pitilessly revealed by the pure light. So will many a life look when the day dawns and the wild riot ends in its unwelcome beams.

The one question for us all, then, will be, Have I lived for Christ and by Him? Let it be the one question for us now, and let it be answered, Yes. Then we shall have at the last a calm confidence, equally far removed from presumption and from dread, which will let us look back on life, though it be full of failures and sins, with peace, and forward with humble hope of the reward that we shall receive from His mercy.

The Triumphant Look Forward

"Henceforth there is laid up for me a crown of righteousness." In harmony with the images of the conflict and the race, the crown here is not the emblem of sovereignty, but of victory, as indeed is almost without exception the case in the New Testament. The idea of the royal dignity of Christians in the future is set forth rather under the emblem of association with Christ on his throne, while the wreath on their brows is the coronal of laurel, "meed of mighty conquerors," or the twine of leaves given to him who, panting, touched the goal. The reward then which is meant by the emblem, whatever be its essence, comes through effort and conflict. "A man . . . is not crowned, except he strive" (2 Tim. 2:5).

That crown, according to other words of Scripture, consists of "life" or "glory"—that is to say, the issue and outcome of believing service and faithful stewardship here is the possession of the true life, which stands in union with God, in measure so great, and in quality so wondrous that it lies on the pure locks of the victors like a flashing diadem, all ablaze with light in a hundred jewels. The completion and exaltation of our nature and characters by the elapse of "life" so sovereign and transcendent that it is "glory" is the consequence of all Christian effort here in the lower levels, where the natural life is always weakness and sometimes shame, and the spiritual life is at the best but a hidden glory and a struggling spark. There is no profit in seeking to gaze into that light of glory so as to discern the shapes of those who walk in it, or the elements of its lambent flames. Enough that in its gracious beauty transfigured souls move as in their native atmosphere! Enough that even our dim vision can see that they have for their companion "one like unto the Son of man" (Rev. 1:13). It is Christ's own life which they share; it is Christ's own glory which irradiates them.

That crown is "a crown of righteousness" in another sense from that in which it is "a crown of life." The latter expression indicates the material, if we may say so, of which it is woven, but the former rather points to the character to which it belongs or is given. Righteousness alone can receive that reward. It is not the struggle or the conflict which wins it, but the character evolved in the struggle; not the work of strenuous service, but the moral nature expressed in these. There is such a congruity between righteousness and the crown of life, that it can be laid on none other head but that of a righteous man, and if it could, all its amaranthine flowers would shrivel and fall when they touched an impure brow. It is, then, the crown of righteousness, as belonging by its very nature to such characters alone.

But whatever is the essential congruity between the character and the crown, we have to remember too that, according to this apostle's constant teaching, the righteousness that clothes us in fair raiment, and has a natural right to the wreath of victory, is a gift, as truly as the crown itself, and is given to us all on condition of our simple trust in Jesus Christ. If we are to be "found of him in peace, without spot, and blameless" (2 Peter 3:14), we must be "found *in* him, not having mine own righteousness . . . but that which is through the faith of Christ" (Phil. 3:9). Toil and conflict, and anxious desire to be true to our responsibilities, will do much for a man, but they will not bring him that righteousness which brings down on the head the crown of life. We must trust to Christ to give us the righteousness in which we are justified, and to give us the righteousness by the working out of which in our life and character we are fitted for that great reward. He crowns our works and selves with exuberant and unmerited honors, but what he crowns is His own gift to us, and His great love must bestow both the righteousness and "the crown."

The crown is given at a time called by Paul "at that day," which is not the near day of his martyrdom, but that of His Lord's appearing. He does not speak of the fullness of the reward as being ready for him at death, but as being "henceforth laid up for him in heaven." So he looks forward beyond the grave. The immediate future after death was to his view a period of blessedness indeed, but not yet full. The state of the dead in Christ was a state of consciousness, a state of rest, a state of felicity, but also a state of expectation. To the full height of their present capacity they who sleep in Jesus are blessed, being still in His embrace. Their spirits pillowed on His heart, nor so sleeping that, like drowsy infants, they know not where they lie so safe, but only sleeping in so much as they rest from weariness, and have closed their eyes to the ceaseless turmoil of this fleeting world, and are lapped about forever with the sweet, unbroken consciousness that they are "present with the Lord" (2 Cor. 5:8). What perfect repose, perfect fruition of all desires, perfect union with the perfect End and Object of all their being, perfect exemption from all sorrow, tumult and sin can bring of blessedness, that they possess in over measure unfailingly. And, in addition, they still know the joy of hope and have carried that jewel with them into another world, for they wait for "the redemption of [the] body" (Rom. 8:23), in the reception of which, "at that day," their life will be filled up to a yet fuller measure and gleam with a more lustrous "glory." Now they rest and wait. Then shall they be crowned.

Nor must self-absorbed thoughts be allowed to bound our anticipations of that future. It is no solitary blessedness to which Paul looked forward. Alone in his dungeon, alone before his judge when "no man stood with" (2 Tim. 4:16) him, soon to be alone in his martyrdom, he leaps up in spirit at the thought of the mighty crowd among whom he will stand in that day, on every head a crown, in every heart the same love to the Lord whose life is in them all and makes them all one. So we may cherish the hope of a social heaven. Man's course begins in a garden, but it ends in a city. The final condition will be the perfection of human society. There all who love Christ will be drawn together, and old ties, broken for a little while here, be reknit in yet holier form, never to be parted more.

Ah, friends, the all-important question for each of us is how may we have such a hope, like a great sunset light shining into the western windows of our souls? There is but one answer—Trust Christ. That is enough. Nothing else is. Is your life built on Jesus Christ? Are you trusting your salvation to Him? Are you giving Him your love and service? Does your life bear looking at today? Will it bear His looking at in death? Will it bear His looking at in Judgment?

If you can humbly say, to me to live is Christ, then is it well. Living by Him we may fight and conquer, may win and obtain. Living by Him, we may be ready quietly to lie down when the time comes, and may have all the future filled with the blaze of a great hope that glows brighter as the darkness thickens. That peaceful hope will not leave us until consciousness fails. Then, when it has ceased to guide us, Christ Himself will lead us, scarcely knowing where we are, through the waters; when we open our half-bewildered eyes in brief wonder, the first thing we see will be His welcoming smile. His voice will say, as a tender surgeon might to a little child waking after an operation, "It is all over." We lift our hands wondering and find wreaths on our poor brows. We lift our eyes, and lo! all about us a crowned crowd of conquerors,

> And with fine morn those angel faces smile
> Which we have loved long since, and lost awhile.

The Days of Our Years

Joseph Parker (1830–1902) was one of England's most popular preachers. Largely self-educated, Parker had pulpit gifts that soon moved him into leadership among the Congregationalists. He was a fearless and imaginative preacher who attracted both common people and the aristocracy, and he was particularly a "man's preacher." His *People's Bible* is a collection of the shorthand reports of the sermons and prayers Parker delivered as he preached through the entire Bible in seven years (1884–1891). He pastored the Poultry Chapel, London, later called the City Temple, from 1869 until his death.

This sermon was taken from *The People's Bible,* volume 12, published in 1900 by Hazell, Watson, and Viney, London.

JOSEPH PARKER

4

The Days of Our Years

The days of our years are threescore years and ten. (Psalm 90:10)

ALMIGHTY GOD, WE BLESS Thee that, though we are always dying, yet we cannot die: Thou hast given us immortality in our Lord Jesus Christ, and though the flesh must fall into the grave, yet shall our spirits rise and praise Thee in other worlds, duration without end. This is our hope, and sometimes it is our agony, for are we not now in the wilderness? are not the enemies abundant? do they not come upon us at unexpected times? and is not our immortality somewhile threatened by foes we cannot repel? Sometimes we long to escape these narrow boundaries of time and these limitations of sense, that we may enter into the complete liberty, the glorious freedom, of the sinless kingdom. Give us patience, help us to wait as men who would gladly go but are remaining here to do the Lord's will. Save us from all repining discontentment and bitterness of soul, give unto us the deep rest of faith, the sweet and tender peace of assured acceptance with God. In all things fill us with the Spirit of our Lord Jesus Christ: He is Thy Son, He is the living Vine; may we be in that living Vine as living branches, bringing forth much fruit, so that Thou mayest be satisfied. We bless Thee for all Thy care: we cannot tell where it begins, we know not where it ends; we cannot lay a line upon the measure thereof, nor can we count its innumerable instances. Behold our life is a witness of Thy care, and we daily testify to the presence of Thy Spirit in our life, working out for us ways we could not have carved for ourselves and giving us solutions infinitely beyond our own sagacity. Let Thy word dwell in us richly; a living word, a word so deep, so high, so full of music and all hopeful voices, a word that is a word of light, illuminating the darkness and making all things beautiful. Sanctify to us our sorrows: may our tears be the showers that water the roots of our joys; may we know that Thou dost not willingly afflict the children of men; teach us the mission and the power of discipline; may we remember that we are the creatures, not the creators, of the universe, and, being such, may we humbly bow and yield to Thee the homage of loving trust, knowing that Thou doest all things well. Turn our hair white with age, break down our backs with heavy burdens and lame us in every limb we have; take the roof from above our heads and the bread from our tables and the water out of the channel that flows by the house-side—but take not Thy Holy Spirit from us. The Lord has the little children here and at home: set a child in the midst of us to teach us the mystery of Thy kingdom, and rebuke us in all our greatness and pride and ability and cleverness—teach us that our hope and our heaven are to be found in the meekness and charity and nobleness and self-sacrifice of Jesus Christ, in whose great, sweet Name we pray. Amen.

The days of our years are threescore years and ten. (Psalm 90:10)

On hearing this statement some may wonder that so well-known a fact should be used as a text. It is just because it is so well-known, and, indeed, so universally admitted, that we wish to see what practical use can be made of it. So far as the fact itself is concerned, there is no opposition or difficulty among us. We receive the text with an assenting sigh. We bow our heads in homage to the tyrant death, knowing that it is useless to bruise our soft hands against his iron scepter. In childhood we laughed at him as a fiction, in manhood we forgot him as a concealed ghost, in advancing age we accost him with reluctant respect, and offer him the grudged hospitality of mourning and sighing, with more or less of articulate distress and lamentation. We know our span; it is but a handbreadth, and it shortens as we measure it. All this is freely and universally admitted, but we wish to ask what kind of conduct ought to be based upon these solemn admissions. Let us grope, or find our way, little by little, from that which is admitted to that which is revealed, and which stands as a perpetual challenge of our attention and a constant appeal to our confidence.

Let us first of all look at our life a little in detail. "The days of our years are threescore years and ten." There is more sound than reality in that statement. We do not live seventy years, though we die on our seventy-first anniversary. The figures are illusory. Take from the seventy years some five years of more or less irresponsible infancy, and the figure drops to sixty-five. From sixty-five subtract one-third of itself as spent in sleep, and the figure drops to some forty-three years, or a little more than five hundred sixteen little months. That is, assuming that we live out the whole string of the seventy years. But let us take the obviously too high average of human life; at fifty years make the same deductions, and we small find the average of human life reduced to some thirty years, or three hundred sixty short, swiftly passing months. It is but a breath, and just over it there glows a heaven and there burns a hell. Into that matter we do not now enter. But it is plainly before us that we have a certain portion of time to spend upon the earth, and we cannot be sure that any one of us will ever spend it. The breath we are now drawing may be our last. There is no guarantee of health, there is no surety given to us that we shall always have a clear intellect, a penetrating eye, a comprehensive mind. At any moment man may be deprived of this. He is followed by packs of wolves he cannot satisfy. On the right hand is an abyss; on the left hand is also an abyss. Many a time in the sky there are lowering clouds. What is man to be and to do within this little span of about three hundred sixty months?

We are told that wise men know exactly from time to time where their money is. They know what money they have, and they know where to find it or how to account for it. We should be as exact in measuring and accounting for our time as we are in respect to our money. Let us try to get at the religious use of time, and hold ourselves as the treasurers of the costliest jewel that can be committed to the care of creatures. "The days of our years are threescore years and ten." Man comes forth as a flower and is cut down. He flees also as a shadow and continues not. See then that you walk circumspectly, not as fools, but as wise, redeeming the time—literally, buying up the opportunity, buying up the chance—for the days are evil.

This course of reflection might easily become so misapplied as to lead to most mischievous results. We must, therefore, presently wholly change the tone. A foolish man hearing this might be led to measure everything by his own individual life, and thus never attempt any work except that of the most narrow and selfish kind. His dreary program would read thus: "I am to be here at the best for some six hundred months; they are flying and perishing whilst I count them. I will buy me a Bible and retire to some mountain cave, and I will sit down and read it again and again until the months be gone. I will commit it all to memory; I will enter into no enterprises; I will venture nothing; I will have no high aspirations, no broad lines of work, no purposes that reach farther than the sunset of the present day—what is the use of it all? I might be gone at any moment; I will therefore spend my life in sighs, and the sooner the end comes the better." This would not be religion; it would be insanity. We are not to base our service on the narrow period of our individual existence. We are to remember that as the universe is larger than any star that shines within it, so humanity is larger than any of the personalities that people it. We are to base our conduct upon the broadest conceptions of human life and human destiny.

Let me remind you that though life is short, yet it is immortal; both the statements are true and are therefore reconcilable. The leaves of every summer fall and die, but the great forests fatten and strengthen, and wave in the winds of centuries. The king dies, the kingdom gets younger every day that lives a true life and sucks its juice from the heart of God. The preacher becomes an old man, withers and dies, and his pulpit sees him no more. But the ministry is immortal, the Word of God abides and is proclaimed forever. An individual man dies and can no more be found than can the knell that dies upon his grave, yet humanity continues—continues building its cities, its temples and towers, weaving and spinning, carving and singing, going with a high joy, as if no grave had ever been cut in the breast of the green earth. We are not, therefore, to mope and moan about our own little day. We are not to lock ourselves up in the little prison of the uncertainty of our own existence. We are not to sit down and read the Bible until death tells us that it is time to go. We have to take in all the world as if it were our business to look after it. We must be inspired by our immortality, not discouraged by our frailty. Young man, you take your start from either of these two divergent points. You can make yourselves old men in an hour by reckoning upon your fingers the number of months you have to live, or you can start under the inspiration of your immortality and say the work that you leave uncompleted will be carried on by others. You can lose your individuality in the great light, as the stars drop away into invisibleness when the firmament is ready to receive the infinite luster of the one orb that can fill it from bound to bound. It is, therefore, to challenge your immortality that I now address you. It is not to make you go to the grave to weep there, but to go to your work, to live in the endless, not to die in the limited and narrow sphere of threescore years and ten.

It was thus that Jesus lived. He died before He had lived out half His seventy years, yet He never died at all. He said: "Pull down what temple you like, that is good, and I will build it again: you cannot pull down God's temples except that they may be rebuilt and enlarged." While the enemy had Him, the one on the left shoulder and the other on the right, and were hurrying Him away to kill Him, He turned His head over His shoulder, as it were, and said, "Lo, I am with you alway, even unto the end of the world" (Matt. 28:20).

Some are in pain and distress by reason of thinking much upon the brevity of life, they have been looking at one side only of a very solemn subject. We ask you now to rise from your perusal of the brevity of life to ponder the fact that this life is but the porch that opens upon immortality. Poetry hardly trifling with history has sometimes touched us to the very blood upon this point. The warrior dies, and says, "I am glad it is all over so far as I am concerned. I wish I had never entered into the war. I care not now what becomes of it."

> The war, that for a space did fail,
> Now trebly thundering, swelled the gate,
> And—Stanley! was the cry;
> A light on Marmion's visage spread,
> And fired his glazing eye:
> With dying hand above his head
> He shook the fragment of a blade,
> And shouted Victory!

That is the man to lead armies to inspire nations, to consolidate churches—the man who does not say, "I care not whether it is victory or defeat," but who in his last breath says "Victory." Trust such men, and not those who write threnodies upon human life as little, mean, narrow, and perishable, instead of being great, noble, and immortal.

The two men now being bound to that stake in Oxford are called Ridley and Latimer. In five minutes the fire will leap upon them and they will be killed. Said one to the other, just as the fire was being lighted, "Brother, we shall light such a candle in England today as shall never be put out." These were not men who moped over their threescore years and ten, who sighed themselves away into decorous oblivion, who lived little narrow, respectable lives nowhere, and finally went into nothing. They were men who made England—who made heaven almost. Their very names are inspirations, and must not, cannot, be forgotten.

So Christ brought life and immortality to light. The psalmist wrote: "The days of our years are threescore years and ten." Christ said: "I came not to destroy the law, but to fulfil it. In these threescore years and ten I will find enough for your immortality." He says, "Sit down." He takes the years, breaks them with His hand, and lo! the seventy loaves spread out into an infinity of banqueting, and in this poor little germ life of mine he found the beginning and the spring of duration long continued as God's own.

Let me remind you further that though life is short, yet it is rich, and that is a consideration that invests life with responsibility. We must do the more on that account. Everything is made ready to our hands. There seems now to be nothing else to be done in the way of invention or of general civilization. We are debtors to the past. We must consider how we can be the creditors of the future. Our forefathers labored. We have entered into their labors. Are we going to be content with them, or are we going to see what can be done to prepare for a great posterity? We now say that money is not so valuable as it was fifty years ago. If you tell your friends what your old father lived upon half a century since, they will say, "That is all very well, but a sovereign then went as far, perhaps, as two sovereigns will go now, so it is no use your basing any economical laws upon such precedents as these." There is sense in that criticism. But what is true of money is exactly untrue of time. Time fifty years ago and time today are not to be compared; they are to be contrasted. We can do fifty times the work that could be done centuries ago in this very country. The library stands ready for the scholar; the steamship is awaiting the traveler; the earth is torn into mines and shafts for the scientific explorer; the telescope is turned toward the heavens and asks for the exploring eye to use it. What chances are ours! It shall be more tolerable for Tyre and Sidon in the day of judgment than for us if we be faithless to our obligations. With telegraphs, telephones, and instruments of all kinds, with inventions of machinery the most subtle and wonderful, with all kinds of timesaving contrivances, to tell us that our seventy years are no longer than the seventy years of the psalmist is to tell us what our own consciousness contradicts, and our own experience denies and repels. If he died at seventy, and we die at the same nominal period of time, we have had the chance of living fifty lives for his one.

What are you doing? What use are you making of the great facilities which are offered to you on every hand? Are you as slow as ever? Are you going to read about the threescore years and ten as if they were figures that could be arithmetically measured? There is a moral measurement, there is a scientific measurement, there is a spiritual measurement, and it is to that higher measurement that we now call you. I cannot allow myself to say that I have only seventy years to live. It is true, arithmetically, but broadly it is false. I have a thousand years to live, and when the psalmist and I meet at the great audit, and he hands us what he has done with his seventy years, I must require angels to help me to lift the burden of my conquests, if I have been a good and faithful servant.

With all this wealth of life, inventions, machinery, libraries, schools, opportunities of all kinds, with all these unreckonable riches of civilization, we are still conscious of a gnawing and intolerable want. Civilization has increased the pungency of that necessity. If civilization had done less we might have thought it could have done more, and we might have been tempted to wait for it. We might have said, "Give civilization time, and she will find the healing plant. She will bring up the golden store that will drive all poverty away. She will fetch the sage from far-off lands that will solve every problem, illuminate every mystery, unloosen every chain. Give her time and she will find the balm to lull my brain to rest and give me the freedom that comes of profound and renewing sleep." Civilization has exhausted itself. There is nothing more possible to civilization except in the matter of degree. You cannot put your finger down upon one thing and say, "Civilization has not attempted this yet." It may not have gone to the full length which it is possible to overtake, but civilization has refined our houses, given us education, dispelled many prejudices, gathered around us riches of all kinds. Civilization has put pictures upon our walls, songs into our mouths, filled our houses with musical instruments, made everything beautiful and rich. Yet we have covered up a worm that dies not with most charming flowers, with most beautiful coverings of all imaginable kinds. The one thing our civilization has not touched in us is our sin. We have seen pictures and have gone home to lay our head upon thorns. We have heard music, an eloquent lie, and have fallen down on bruised knees to utter a sobbing cry for pardon.

So Jesus Christ still keeps His place in civilization. He begins where others end. Where they cry from exhaustion He puts on His strength. Where the mystery bewilders and blinds them, He dispels it by many a shaft of light. He is the propitiation for my sins. He stands between me and God, and O, mystery of love, He stands between me and Himself. For He too is Judge, and the sentence of life and death is upon His lips. He knows my days—He comforts me with many a promise. He knows my sin—He says He came to reply to its agony and to destroy its power. He knows my weariness, and He promises me rest in His own great heart. Let this be said about Him—which can be said of no other man—He met the world's want, in words if not in realities. Say what we will about realities, this Man mentioned the very thing we need most. He says, "You want life?" Yes, that is true. "You want rest?" Yes, above all things we want rest. "You feel hunger?" Yes, a gnawing hunger. "You are thirsty?" Yes, aflame, afire with thirst. "Then," says He, "I have mentioned your necessities. I will address myself to their direct and immediate and complete supply." As a poetical conception, taking that limited view only, the Carpenter's Son stands above kings and crowned ones of every name and suggests what they had not ventured to dream.

"The days of our years are threescore years and ten." We look on one side and hardly think them worth living at all. We put stones one upon the other and a wind blows them down. We say, "I will go into this or that city, and abide there a year, and buy and sell and get gain," and lo! on the starting day we are too ill to move. We are consumed before the moth, the insect is an antagonist we cannot conquer. We see the grave of our friend, and written at the bottom of it is, "Yours will be dug tomorrow." We feel how mean is life and how poor is the measure of our time. Then it is that we want a man to come to us with revelations of a higher kind, to speak to us of possibilities that do not lie within the arithmetical compass of our seventy years.

My life—so frail that an insect can consume it, a lamp, flickering so that a breath might blow it out—that is my life in itself. But hidden in Christ, hidden in God, hidden in the living Vine, part of the fellowship divine, "I can the darkening universe defy to quench my immortality, or shake my trust in God."

The Sorrows of the Bereaved Spread Before Jesus

Jonathan Edwards (1703-1758) was a Congregational preacher, a theologian and a philosopher, possessing one of the greatest minds ever produced on the American continent. He graduated with highest honors from Yale in 1720, and in 1726 was ordained and served as co-pastor with his grandfather, Solomon Stoddard, in Northfield, Massachusetts. When Stoddard died in 1729, Edwards became sole pastor, a position he held until doctrinal disagreements with the church led to his resignation in 1750. He played a key role in The Great Awakening (1734-44) and is perhaps best known for his sermon "Sinners in the Hands of an Angry God."

This sermon was taken from *The Works of Jonathan Edwards,* volume 2, published by Banner of Truth Trust in 1976.

JONATHAN EDWARDS

5

The Sorrows of the Bereaved Spread Before Jesus

And his disciples came, and took up the body, and buried it, and went and told Jesus. (Matthew 14:12)

CONCERNING THESE WORDS I would observe three things.

First, on what occasion that was, that we have an account of in the text. It was on occasion of the death of John the Baptist, who was a person whose business it had been to preach the gospel of the kingdom of God. He was a minister of Jesus Christ and had been improved to do great service. He was an instrument of much good to many in Judea and Jerusalem in his lifetime. He was cruelly murdered by Herod at the instigation of Herodias, having exposed himself to her malice by faithfully reproving them for their incestuous wickedness.

Second, we may observe who the persons were spoken of in the text. They were those that had been the disciples of John the Baptist. They were those that had sat at his feet to hear him preach the gospel, that were his constant followers, that were with him as those that received great benefit by his ministry and were, as it were, his children.

And third, we may observe their behavior on this occasion, consisting in two things.

One, that whereby they showed their regard to the remains of the deceased, they *took up the body, and buried it*. It had been used in a barbarous manner by others that had also been his hearers and were under special obligations to have treated him with honor. They cruelly murdered him by severing his head from his body. His head was carried in a charger to Herodias that she, instead of paying that respect that was due to the remains of so venerable a person, might have her malice and cruelty gratified by such a spectacle, and that she might thence take occasion to insult the dead. While that part of the dead body was thus used by Herodias, his disciples, out of respect and honor to their master and teacher, decently interred the rest.

And two, that which they did, consequent on this, for God's glory and their own good, they *went and told Jesus*. Him they knew to be one that their master John, while he lived, had testified a great regard to. Jesus was He whose forerunner John was. Jesus was the One of whom he had preached and of whom he had said, "Behold the Lamb of God, which taketh away the sin of the world" (John 1:29). And, "This is he of whom I said, After me cometh a man which is preferred before me" (v. 30). And Jesus was the One of whom he saw and bare record that *this is the Son of God*. And probably they knew that Christ was one that had put great honor upon John their teacher in his lifetime. For He, though He was the Son of God, and John's Maker and Savior, yet came to him to be baptized of him, and had said of him, "Among them that are born of women, there hath not risen a greater than John the Baptist" (Matt. 11:11).

It was now a sorrowful time with John's disciples when they were thus bereaved of him whose teachings they had sat under. And the manner of his death was doubtless very grievous to them. They were like a company of sorrowful, distressed, bereaved children. What do they do in their sorrows, but go to Jesus with their complaint. The first thing that they do, after paying proper regard to the remains of their dear master, is to go to Christ to spread their case before Him, seeking comfort and help from Him. Thus they sought their own benefit.

And probably one end of their immediately going and telling Jesus was that He, being informed of it, might conduct Himself accordingly, as His wisdom should direct for the interest of His own kingdom. When so great a person as John the Baptist, the forerunner of Christ, was thus martyred, it was a great event in which the common cause, in which both Christ and he were engaged, was greatly concerned. It was therefore fit that He that was at the head of the whole affair should be informed of it for His future conduct in the affairs of His kingdom. And accordingly we find that Jesus seems immediately to be influenced in His conduct by these tidings. As you may see in the next verse: "When Jesus heard of it, he departed thence by ship into a desert place apart" (Matt. 14:13). Thus John's disciples sought God's glory.

The observation from the words that I would make the subject of my discourse at this time, is this: When anyone is taken away by death that has been eminent in the work of the gospel ministry, such as are thereby bereaved should go and spread their calamity before Jesus.

Though in handling this subject I might particularly speak to several propositions that are contained in this observation, and many things might profitably be insisted on under it if there were room for it within the compass of a sermon. Yet I shall only give the reasons of the doctrine, and then hasten to the application.

The following reasons may be given why, in case of such an awful dispensation of providence, those that are concerned in it and bereaved by it, should go and spread their sorrows before Jesus:

1. Christ is one that is ready to pity the afflicted. It is natural for persons that are bereaved of any that are dear to them, and for all under deep sorrow, to seek some that they may declare and lay open their griefs to, that they have good reason to think will pity them and have a fellow feeling with them of their distress. The heart that is full of grief wants vent and desires to pour out its complaint, but it seeks a compassionate friend to pour it out before.

Christ is such a one, above all others. He of old, before His incarnation, manifested Himself full of compassion toward His people, for that is Jesus that is spoken of in Isaiah 63:9: "In all their affliction he was afflicted, and the angel of his presence saved them: in his love and in his pity he redeemed them; and he bare them, and carried them all the days of old." And when He was upon earth in His state of humiliation, He was the most wonderful instance of a tender, pitiful, compassionate spirit that ever appeared in the world. How often are we told of His having compassion on one and another. "Then Jesus called his disciples unto him, and said, I have compassion on the multitude" (Matt. 15:32). So He had compassion on the man possessed with devils. "Go home to thy friends, and tell them how great things the Lord hath done to thee, and hath had compassion on thee" (Mark 5:19). So we read of his pitying the mother that was bereaved of her son (Luke 7:13). There we have an account, when Christ went into the city of Nain and met the people carrying out a dead man, the only son of his mother that was a widow, that when He saw her He had compassion on her. So when the two blind men that sat by the wayside cried to Jesus as He passed by saying, "Have mercy on us, O Lord, thou Son of David" (Matt. 20:30), we read that Jesus had compassion on them. So we read of His being moved with compassion. "And Jesus went forth, and saw a great multitude, and was moved with compassion toward them" (Matt. 14:14). His speeches to His disciples were full of compassion, especially those that He uttered a little before His death, of which we have an account in chapters 13–16 of John. His miracles were almost universally deeds of pity to persons under affliction.

And seeing such a pitiful heart appeared in Him on all occasions, no wonder that John's disciples, when bereaved of their dear guide and teacher, and their hearts were full of sorrow, came to Him for pity. This likewise induced Mary and Martha to come and fall down, pouring out their tears at Jesus' feet when their dear brother Lazarus was dead. Other Jews came to comfort them before Jesus came, whom they little regarded, but when they heard that Jesus was come, they soon go and spread their sorrows before Him. They were assured that He would pity them. Their expectation was not frustrated, for He was most tenderly affected and moved at their tears. We are told that on that occasion "he groaned in the spirit, and was troubled" (John 11:33). And when He came to the grave, it is observed, and a special note seems to be set upon it, that "Jesus wept" (v. 35).

He was one that wept with those that wept. Indeed, it was mere pity that brought Him into the world and induced Him not only to shed tears but to shed His blood. He poured out His blood as water on the earth out of compassion to the poor, miserable children of men. And when do we ever read of any one person coming to Him when on earth with a heavy heart, or under any kind of sorrow or distress for pity or help, but what met with a kind and compassionate reception?

And He has the same compassion now He is ascended into glory. There is still the same encouragement for bereaved ones to go and spread their sorrows before Him.

Afflicted persons love to speak of their sorrows to them that have had experience of affliction and know what sorrow is. But there is none on earth or in heaven that ever had so much experience of sorrow as Christ. Therefore He knows how to pity the sorrowful, and especially may we be confident that He is ready to pity those that are bereaved of a faithful minister, because such a bereavement is a calamity that concerns the souls of men. Christ has especially shown His pity to men's souls, for it was chiefly for them that He died. To relieve the miseries of the soul, especially, is it that He has provided. It was from pity to the souls of men that He made that provision for them that He has done, in appointing such an order of men as gospel ministers, and in sending them forth to preach the gospel. It was because He had compassion on men's souls that He has appointed ministers to watch for souls.

2. Christ has purchased all that persons need under such a bereavement. He has purchased all that miserable men stand in need of under all their calamities, and comfort under every sort of affliction. Therefore, His invitation to those that "labour and are heavy laden" (Matt. 11:28) to come to Him for rest may be understood, in the most extensive sense, to extend to those that are "heavy laden" with either natural or moral evil. He has purchased divine cordials and supports for those hearts that are ready to sink. He has purchased all needed comfort and help for the widow and the fatherless. He has purchased a sanctified improvement and fruit of affliction for all such as come to Him and spread their sorrows before Him. He has purchased those things that are sufficient to make up their loss, that are bereaved of a great blessing in an eminent minister of the gospel. It is He that has purchased those divine blessings, those influences and fruits of the Spirit of God, that the work of the ministry is appointed to be the means of. Faithful ministers themselves are

the fruits of His purchase. He has purchased all those gifts and graces whereby ministers do become faithful, eminent, and successful. Therefore when He "ascended up on high, he . . . gave gifts unto men" (Eph. 4:8ff.). So that He has purchased all that is needed to make up for the loss that is sustained by the death of an eminent minister.

3. Christ is able to afford all the help that is needed in such a case. His power and His wisdom are as sufficient as His purpose and answerable to His compassions. By the bowels of His mercies, the love and tenderness of His heart, He is disposed to help those that are in affliction. His ability is answerable to His disposition. He is able to support the heart under the heaviest sorrows and to give light in the greatest darkness. He can divide the thickest cloud with beams of heavenly light and comfort. He is one that gives songs in the night and turns the shadow of death into the morning. He has power to make up the loss of those that are bereaved by the death of the most eminent minister. His own presence with the bereaved is sufficient. If the great Shepherd and Bishop of souls be present, how much more is this than enough to supply the want of any under shepherd! And then He is able to furnish others with like gifts and graces for that work.

Persons under sorrowful bereavements are ready to go and lay open their sorrows to them that they think will be ready to pity them, though they know they can but pity them and cannot help them. How much more is here in such a case to induce us to go to Jesus, who is not only so ready to pity, but so able to help, able abundantly more than to fill up the breach, and able to turn all our sorrows into joy!

4. The consideration of the special office of Christ and the work that He has undertaken for His people should engage them to go and spread such a calamity as the bereavement of a faithful and eminent minister before Him. For He is the head of the body, the great Shepherd of the sheep, and Lord of the harvest that has undertaken the care of the whole church, and has the absolute government of it in His hands, and the supreme disposal and management of all ecclesiastical affairs. To whom belongs the care of the universal church, and every part of it, with respect to its supply with such guides, officers, and

ordinances as it stands in need of. In case of bereavement of an eminent minister, it was He that sent forth such a minister, appointed Him his charge, and furnished him for his work, continued and assisted him in it, and in His own time removed him. It is He that, in such a case, by His office, has the care of filling up the vacancy, furnishing, establishing, and assisting successors, and supplying all the wants of bereaved churches. It is surely therefore suitable and natural to go to Him in such a case and spread such a calamity before Him.

Application

I come now to apply what has been said to the sorrowful occasion of our being thus assembled at this time, even the death of that aged servant of God, who has long been eminent in the work of the gospel ministry in this place.

There are many that may well look on themselves as nearly concerned in this awful providence and sharers in the bereavement, all of whom should be directed by this doctrine to go and spread their affliction before Jesus—the compassionate, all-sufficient Head of the church and Savior of the body, the merciful and faithful High Priest who knows how to pity the afflicted.

And particularly it now becomes and concerns you who belong to this church and congregation, that are bereaved of your aged and eminent pastor and father, who has so long been a great blessing to you, now to go and tell Jesus.

The disciples of John, spoken of in the text, were those that were ordinarily under his instruction and were his constant hearers, as it has been with you with respect to your aged pastor, who is now taken from you. Therefore be exhorted to do as they did. Do not think that you have finished your duty when you have taken up his body and buried it, and have shown respect to his memory and remains at his funeral. This is the least part of your duty. That which mainly concerns you under this awful providence is between Christ and your own souls.

God has now taken away from you an able and faithful minister of the New Testament, one that had long been a father to you, and a father in our Israel. A person of uncommon natural abilities and distinguished learning, a great divine of very comprehensive knowledge and of a solid, accurate judgment. Judiciousness and wisdom were eminently his character. He was one of eminent gifts, qualifying him for all parts of the work of the ministry. There appeared a savor of holiness in his exercise of those gifts in public and private, so that he improved them as a servant of Christ, and a man of God. He was not negligent of the talents which his Lord had committed to him. You need not be told with what constant diligence he improved them, how studious at home, and how laborious in his public work. He ever devoted himself to the work to which he is called. The ministry which he had received of the Lord he took heed to fulfill and pursued it with a constant, steadfast, even mind through all its difficulties.

You know his manner of addressing heaven in his public prayers with you and for you. With what sanctity, humility, faith, and fervency he seemed to apply himself to the Father of lights, from time to time, when he stood in this desk as your mouth to God, and interceding for you, pleading with God through the grace and merits of a glorious Mediator. And you know his manner of applying himself to you, when he came to you, from time to time, in the name of the Lord.

In his public ministry, he mainly insisted on the most weighty and important things of religion. He was eminently an evangelical preacher. Evangelical subjects seemed to be his delight. Christ was the great subject of his preaching. He much insisted on those things that did nearly concern the essence and power of religion. He had a peculiar faculty of judiciously and clearly handling the doctrines he insisted on, and treating properly whatever subject he took in hand, and of selecting the most weighty arguments and motives to enforce and set home those things that concern Christian experience and practice. His subjects were always weighty, and his manner of treating them peculiarly happy, showing the strength and accuracy of his judgment and ever breathing forth the spirit of piety and a deep sense of the things he delivered on his heart. His sermons were none of them mean, but were all solid, wise compositions. His words were none of them vain, but all were weighty.

And you need not be told with what weight the welfare of your souls seemed to lie on his heart, and how he instructed, reproved, warned, and exhorted you, with all authority and with a fatherly tender concern for your eternal good. And with what wisdom he presided in the house of God and guided its affairs, and also counseled and directed you in private under your particular soul exercises and difficulties. You know how he has brought you up (for most of you have been trained up from your childhood under his ministry), with what authority, judgment, prudence, and steadiness he has conducted you, as well as meekness and gentleness. You know his manner of going in and out among you. You know how exemplary his walk and conversation has been, with what gravity, judgment, and savor of holiness he has walked before you as a man of God.

You have enjoyed great advantages for your souls' good under his ministry. That you had such a minister was your privilege and your honor. He has been an ornament to the town of Hatfield. His presence and conversation among you has been both profitable and pleasant; for though it was such as did peculiarly command awe and respect, yet it was, at the same time, humble and condescending. It tended both to instruct and entertain those that he conversed with. As a wise man, and endued with knowledge, he showed out of a good conversation his works with meekness of wisdom.

But now it has pleased a holy God to take him away from you. You will see his face and hear his voice no more in the land of the living. You will no more have the comfort and benefits of his presence with you and the exercise of his ministry among you.

Therefore now go to Jesus, the Supreme Head of the church and Bishop of souls. Your pastor is dead and will not live again until the last day. But Christ, the chief Shepherd, though He was dead, is now alive! And behold, He lives forevermore. He ever lives to provide for His church, and to guide and feed His flock. Go to that Jesus whom your deceased pastor preached, and to whom he earnestly invited you while he lived, and give thanks for the many blessings you enjoyed in him. Remember how you have received and heard, and hold fast that no man take your crown. Go and humble yourselves also before Him, that you made no better improvement of the ministry of your pastor while he lived. Beg of Him a sanctified improvement of

His awful hand in taking him away. Ask Him to help you to remember his warnings and counsels that you too much slighted while you had them, lest those warnings and counsels cry against you and rise up in judgment against you another day. Ask Him to help you to remember lest you see your pastor, who so affectionately and earnestly and so often and for so long a time continued to exhort you and earnestly prayed for you while he lived, rising up in judgment and bearing testimony against you, declaring how constantly and laboriously he entreated and called upon you, and how obstinately some of you slighted his counsels. Ask Him to help you to remember lest you see him sitting with Christ to judge and condemn you, and adoring his awful justice on your aggravated punishment.

All you that have an interest in Jesus, now go to Him on this occasion, tell Him of your bereavement, and beg of Him that He would not depart from you, but that He would make up His loss in His own immediate presence. Go to Him for your surviving pastor, that He would be with him and furnish him more and more for, and assist him in, that great work that is now wholly devolved upon him. Ask Jesus to make him also a burning and shining light among you, and that you may have of the presence and blessing of Jesus with you and him.

And now, since I am called to speak in the name of Christ on this solemn occasion, I would apply myself to the near relations of the deceased who are especially to be looked upon as the bereaved.

God in His holy providence has taken from you one that has been a great blessing, comfort, and honor to you, and deservedly very dear to you and honored of you. The doctrine we are upon directs you what to do in your present circumstances, namely, to go to Jesus, to go and spread your affliction before an all-sufficient Redeemer.

And particularly I would apply myself to the honored relict, who stood in the nearest relation of any to the deceased, whom God by this awful providence has made a sorrowful widow. Suffer me, honored madam, in your great affliction to exhibit to you a compassionate Redeemer. God has now taken from you that servant of His that was the nearest and best friend you had in this world, that was your wise and prudent guide, your affectionate and pleasant companion, who was so great a blessing while he lived to you and your family and, under Christ, was so much the comfort and support of your life. You see, madam, where your resort must be. Your earthly friends can condole your loss, but cannot make it up to you. We must all confess ourselves to be but miserable comforters. But you may go and tell Jesus, and there you may have both support and reparation. His love and His presence is far beyond that of the nearest and most affectionate earthly friend. Now you are bereaved of your earthly consort, you may go to a spiritual husband and seek His compassion and His company. He is the fountain of all that wisdom and prudence, that piety, that tender affection and faithful care, that you enjoyed in your departed consort. In Him is an infinite fountain of all these things, and of all good. In Him you may have light in your darkness, comfort in your sorrow, and fullness of joy and glory in another world. In Him you may have an everlasting union with your dear, deceased relative in the glorious presence of the same Redeemer, in whose presence is fullness of joy and at whose right hand are pleasures forevermore.

This doctrine also directs the bereaved, afflicted children who are, with hearts full of grief, now mourning over a dear departed father and wondering where to go and what to do. You will no longer have your father's wisdom to guide you, his tender love to comfort and delight you, his affectionate care to guard you and assist you, his pious and judicious counsels to direct you, his holy examples set before you, and his fervent, humble, believing prayers with you and for you.

But in the blessed Jesus, your father's Lord and Redeemer, you may have much more than all those things. Your father's virtues that made him so great a blessing to you were but the image of what is in Christ.

Therefore go to Him in your mourning. Go and tell Jesus, tell a compassionate Savior what has befallen you. Heretofore you have had an earthly father to go to whose heart was full of tenderness to you, but the heart of his Redeemer is much more tender. His wisdom and His love is infinitely beyond that of any earthly parent. Go to Him, and then you will surely find comfort. Go to Him, and you will find that, though you are bereaved, yet you are not left in any want. You will find that all your wants are supplied, all your loss made up, and much more than so.

But here I would particularly, in humility, address myself to my honored fathers, the sons of the deceased, that are improved in the same great work of the gospel ministry or in other public business for the service of their generation. Honored sirs, though it might be more proper for me to come to you for instruction and counsel than to take it upon me to exhort you, yet as I am one that ought to have a fellow-feeling of your affliction and to look on myself as a sharer in it, and as you have desired me to speak in the name of Christ on this occasion, suffer me to mention to you that source of comfort, that infinite fountain of good, one of the larger streams of which has failed by the death of an earthly father, even the blessed Jesus. You will doubtless acknowledge it as an instance of His great goodness to you that you have been the sons of such a father. Being sensible that your reputation and serviceableness in your generation have been, under Christ, very much owing to the great advantages you have been under by his instructions, counsels, and education. And is it not fit that children that have learned of such a faithful servant of Christ and been brought up at his feet, now he is dead, should do as John the Baptist's disciples did, go and tell Jesus? From whom you may receive comfort under your bereavement, and from whom you may receive more of that Spirit that dwelt in him, and greater degrees of those virtues lie derived from Christ to cause you to shine brighter and to make you still greater blessings in your generation. Now death has veiled and hid from sight a star that shone with reflected light, our text and doctrine leads you to the Sun, who has light in Himself and shines with infinite, unfailing brightness. And while you go to Jesus, honored sirs, on this occasion for yourselves, I humbly desire your requests to Him for us the surviving ministers of this county, that He would be with us, now that He has taken from us him that was a father among us.

I next would address myself to the surviving pastor of this church. We may well look upon you, reverend sir, as one in an especial manner concerned in this awful providence and that has a large share in the bereavement. You doubtless are sensible what reason you have to bless God for the advantage you have had in serving in the gospel of Christ, so long as you have done, with the venerable person deceased, as a son with a father enjoying the benefit of his instructions, counsels, and example. And particularly, you will often recollect the affectionate and fatherly counsels he gave you to diligence and faithfulness in your Lord's work, with encouragement of his protection and assistance to carry you through all difficulties, the last evening of his life. And now, dear sir, God has taken him from you, as he took Elijah from Elisha, and as he took John the Baptist, the New Testament Elijah, from his disciples. Therefore now you are directed what to do, namely, *go and tell Jesus* as those disciples did. You have now a great work devolved upon you. You have him no more, who, while he lived, was as a father to you to guide and assist you and take the burden of your great work from you. Therefore you have nowhere else to go but to your great Lord and Master, who has sent you to labor in that part of His vineyard where His aged, and now departed, servant was employed to seek strength and wisdom, and divine influence and assistance from Him, and a double portion of that Spirit that dwelt in your predecessor.

And lastly, the text I am upon may be of direction to us, the surviving ministers of this county, what to do on this sorrowful occasion. God has now taken our father and master from our head. He has removed him that has heretofore, under Christ, been very much our strength that we have been wont to resort to it in difficult cases for instruction and direction, and that used to be among us from time to time in our associations, and that we were wont to behold as the head and ornament of those conventions. Where else can we now go but to Jesus, the ever-living Head of the whole church and Lord of the whole harvest, the Fountain of light, our great Lord and Master, that sends all gospel ministers and on whom they universally depend? Let this awful providence bring us to look to Christ, to seek more of His presence with us and that He would preside as head in our associations. Let it bring us to a more immediate and entire dependence upon Him for instruction and direction in all our difficulties.

Let us on this occasion consider what God has done in this county of late years. It was not many years ago that the county was filled with aged ministers who were our fathers. But our fathers, where are they? What a great alteration is made in a little time in the churches in this part of the land! How frequent of late have been the warnings of this kind that God has given us to prepare to give up our account! Let us go to Jesus and seek grace of Him that we may be faithful while we live, and that He would assist us in our great work, that when we also are called hence, we may give up our account with joy and not with grief, and that hereafter we may meet those of our fathers, who have gone before us in the faithful labors of the gospel, and that we may shine forth with them, as the brightness of the firmament, and as the stars forever and ever.

NOTES

Christ's Delay to Interpose Against Death

John Ker (1819-1886) is little known today, but in his day he was a respected preacher and professor of preaching and pastoral work at the United Free Church Seminary in Glasgow, Scotland. He published two volumes of sermons.

This sermon was taken from the *Sermons First Series,* published in Edinburgh in 1870 by Edmonston and Douglas.

JOHN KER

6

Christ's Delay to Interpose Against Death

> Then when Mary was come where Jesus was, and saw him, she fell down at his feet, saying unto him, Lord, if thou hadst been here, my brother had not died. (John 11:32)

THE WORDS OF MARY are very touching and natural. There is a mingled gush of feeling in them, which she herself would have found it difficult to refer to its different sources. All her grief for her dead brother bursts out afresh at the sight of One who had been so dear a friend to him and to her. Veneration and affection for the Great Master, never so drawn out as in the hour of sorrow, fill her soul. "Mary . . . *fell down* at his feet." Formerly she was willing to *sit* at them. The soul is never so attracted to Christ as amid such desolation—constrained to cling to "a friend that sticketh closer than a brother" (Prov. 18:24).

There is continued confidence in Him, seen in her address, *Lord*. He is still *Lord*, notwithstanding all that had happened. He is still *Lord*, seen in the conviction that an earlier arrival would have brought deliverance, "If thou hadst been here, my brother had not died," and leading to a hope that He was able to help even in this extremity, she could not tell how.

It will be observed that Mary uses the very same words which Martha had already employed in John 11:21. The reason may be that they had often used the words to one another. "If Jesus only *would* come—if Jesus only *had* come, all might be well." But it seems remarkable that Mary does not go on to finish her appeal as Martha did in verse 22, "But I know, that even now, whatsoever thou wilt ask of God, God will give it thee." Was Mary's faith less strong than Martha's? We think not. Mary's sentence was finished in her own heart. She had a more intense and impetuous nature. With its stillness, there was more depth in it, and she cannot give vent to her feelings in words. Tears break in upon and check her utterance, for it is immediately added, "When Jesus therefore saw her weeping" (v. 33). She had fallen at His feet, and her bursting emotion would not allow her to say more, "Lord, if thou hadst been here, my brother had not died, but . . ." and all the faith expressed by Martha, though unuttered by Mary's lips is deep within her soul.

Yet with this faith, there is wonder at the absence of Christ which verges almost on reproach. "Surely there must have been reasons for my Lord's delay while we wept and prayed for His coming, while every morning, and through the long day, our eyes sought the hills where His steps might be first descried. Why so late when this dead brother of mine, and friend of Yours, was sinking to his grave?" "O the hope of Israel, the saviour thereof in time of trouble, why shouldest thou be as a stranger in the land?" (Jer. 14:8).

Such thoughts as these have since passed through many a heart and will do until the world's close. What sore strokes befall us in this matter of death from which the Son of God could easily save us, if His power and His pity be as we are told! They are very natural thoughts, natural above all, when we watch by the deathbed and weep over the dead. They were felt by Mary in Christ's presence, and may be felt by us during His long absence. He has now been away so many long days, and our dead lie buried, and yet He comes not. We shall seek to look at the question in the light which this narrative gives. *First,* there is the strangeness of Christ's delay to interpose against death. *Second,* some reasons that may account for it are suggested by this history. The *first* may give expression to our doubts; the *second,* help our faith.

The Strangeness of Christ's Delay to Interpose Against Death

Let us turn our thoughts to the circumstances around us, as Mary and Martha might to the state of their home in the absence of Christ.

Consider *what death is to the sufferer!* It is no natural change, no happy translation bearing the sign of blessedness on its face, as the departure of unfallen man might have done. It is the end of all earthly sufferings, but, in general, more dreaded than them all. The token of God's displeasure against sin is on it, and the abiding shadow of His first threatening. Man's heart recoils from its accompaniments—the wasting decay or the convulsive agony; the farewell to the only world we have known; the rending asunder of the dearest ties of affection and of those closest friends, body and soul; the dismissal of our nature to the corruption of the grave and to a mysterious eternity.

When we see a friend moving forward to this doom, what means do we not exhaust to save him? When Thomas heard that Lazarus was dead, he said, "Let us also go, that we may die with him" (John 11:16). So did the death of a dear friend touch his sympathetic heart. Yet Christ suffered Lazarus to die. And how many have been struck down by death since, of time most lovely and loving? What warm hearts and noble souls have passed through that great gloom and drunk of that bitter cup—beautiful exceedingly with the beauty of nature and with the grace of the regenerated spirit! What sad thoughts we have sometimes about the bright jewels that lie hidden in death's darkness! We were stricken and stunned when death did not spare them, at the cruel untimeliness, as it seemed, at the fierce remorselessness with which the great enemy seized his prey. And yet when we speak of death, it had no power without Christ's permission: "Lord, if thou hadst been here, my brother had not died."

Consider *what a bereavement death is to the survivors!* In a Christian death it is not the dead who are to be mourned, it is those whom they leave. What anxious days and nights were those after the message had been sent, "Lord, behold, he whom thou lovest is sick!" (v. 3). Their brother is sinking to his grave, as each sun sinks over the western hills, and there is no token of help. Their look seeks the wasting frame, and then seeks the path by which Jesus so often drew near. Has He forgotten His friends, or does He distrust His power? Those who have passed through it know what ages of agony are lived, while the wavering balance is watched and slowly seen to sink against all our struggles and prayers.

And then the anguish of the parting—the dumb despair that cannot find a tear—the hard apathy, like a stone on a grave's mouth, that will not let us feel our way to our loss to weep over it! The slow groping that follows to realize it. The struggle, as if emerging from the stupor of death, to find out what a different world it is to which we have come back. The look behind to years of love which seem so short, cut off from us already by an earthquake's gulf, and strange as if they had never been ours. The look forward to a lonely road through a bleak world from which one blast of desolation has swept the greenness and the blossom! "Lover and friend hast thou put far from me, and mine acquaintance into darkness" (Ps. 88:18). How often has the old wailing cry burst from human hearts, how often the death-scene of Bethany been renewed in the homes of men! The childless mother and the orphan, the wife and sister, lover and friend, have wrestled in agony over the dying and moaned over the dead, and none seemed to listen. They felt there should be power of help somewhere, and writhed toward it. And the appeals remained unanswered. Does it not seem strange? "Lord, if thou hadst been here, my brother had not died."

Consider *what a ground of reproach death has furnished to the enemies of Christ!* There was no want of unbelieving Jews in Bethany to take advantage of Christ's absence in this crisis. Some of them said, "Could not this man, which opened the eyes of the blind, have caused that even this man should not have died?" (John 11:37). But beyond this more friendly question, there must have been hard thoughts of unbelief—the resolve to read all Christ's past by this delay. Whisperings and shakings of the head there were, no doubt, in plenty, breaking out into open speech, as still He came not. "These wonderful histories and great promises have been brought to a decisive test, and Lazarus, the friend of Jesus, must die and be buried like all of us. Let Him deliver him, seeing He delighted in him." It must have added vinegar to the gall of those sisters' grief to hear the taunt. Their faith was assailed from without, when it was questioned by their hearts within. Something like the feeling of the psalmist must have been theirs: "My tears have been my meat day and night, while they continually say unto me, Where is thy God?" (Ps. 42:3).

A longer interval of death has allowed time for a louder concert of reproach. As we look into the grave after each new occupant, all is hushed. There is no motion in the dead, no breath in the sky to whisper of a coming dawn. And men of carnal sense gather around and set their seal upon the grave: "Where is the promise of his coming? for since the fathers fell asleep, all things continue as they were from the beginning of the creation" (2 Peter 3:4). Even the Christian heart feels as if there were something strange in the way in which Christ abides out of sight and moves not a step for all the scorn. It wearies for some interposition to vindicate His claim. "Arise, O God, plead thine own cause: remember how the foolish man reproacheth thee daily . . . the tumult of those that rise up against thee increaseth continually" (Ps. 74:22-23).

There is still another way in which the strangeness of the delay may strike us—when we turn our thoughts from our own circumstances, to Christ, as the sisters of Bethany did, and when we consider the just expectations we have of interposition from Him.

We believe that *Christ is fully aware of our need*. When a friend fails us through innocent ignorance, we do not blame him. What pains us is his persistent absence when he knows our extremity. So soon as these sisters apprehended danger, they sent the message to Jesus, "Lord, behold, he whom thou lovest is sick!" They appear to have added no request to it. "It is enough if Jesus knows—this will bring Him to our side." And when He did not come, and day after day passed on, we can imagine the messenger questioned and requestioned how he gave his message, and how the Master seemed to apprehend it. "Could He but see this wasting frame and our fears, He would not fail us."

Whatever Martha and Mary thought of the knowledge of Christ, it is our faith that He understands all our need. When we send up the prayer, "Lord, behold, he whom thou lovest is sick," it is only because He will be inquired of by us. With the omniscience of the Son of God, He sees the dwellers upon earth, and, with the experience of the Son of Man, He comprehends their sorrows. "If you only knew what I suffer," we say to a friend, as if his conception of it would call out a sympathy that would bear us up in its hands. Yet Christ knows it all. He can draw nearer than the nearest, feel the palpitating heart, read the anguish we cannot utter—and his foot does not step forward to the rescue. Is it not strange?

We believe, further, that *Christ has full power to interpose*. The mourners of Bethany express their conviction of it, "I know, that even now, whatsoever thou wilt ask of God, God will give it thee" (John 11:22). And Christ expresses it in his prayer to his Father, "I knew that thou hearest me always" (v. 42). For it is our faith that He has not only the omnipotence of divinity, but the moral right and power from having paid the ransom price. When He said upon His cross, "It is finished" (19:30), God raised Him from the dead, and set Him at His own right hand in heavenly places, as the sign that the way is clear to abolish death—to destroy it forever in regard to all who look to Him as the Resurrection and the Life. Who, in this, could resist His will? The keys of the unseen world and of death hang at His girdle. That He should be so slow to put His authority into exercise, when such tides of suffering would be rolled back and such a flood of overwhelming joy set in, must occasion to many Christians strange thoughts.

For, last of all, on this part of the subject, *we cannot doubt the desire of Christ to interpose*. The evangelist is careful to remind us of this feature of it, "Now Jesus loved Martha, and her sister, and Lazarus. When he had heard therefore that he was sick, he abode two days still in the same place where he was" (11:5–6). It is a strange *therefore* which conjoins such love and seeming indifference. Then follows that account of the conduct of Christ which is filled with such everlasting consolation to a dying world, and which yet suggests so many wondering questions, "When Jesus therefore saw her weeping, and the Jews also weeping which came with her, he groaned in the spirit, and was troubled, and said, Where have ye laid him? They said unto him, Lord, come and see. *Jesus wept*" (vv. 33–35).

But, if He felt so deeply for His friends, why did He not come sooner to comfort them and interpose in their behalf? And, if He meant now to interpose, and knew what He was about to do at the grave of Lazarus, why should He weep? However we may answer such questions, we must never doubt that the tears of Christ were not seeming, but deeply real, and that the groans of His spirit came from true sympathy with human sorrow. He wept as those mourners did, although He might weep with "larger, other eyes than theirs"—weeping, not with *them* only, but with mourners without number, as He looked abroad over the world and down through all time. He wept with every bereaved heart, and with each solitary soul which thinks that its way is hid from the Lord, and its judgment passed over by its God. Yet here our perplexity still rises. If so He feels, and if He has power and right to interpose, why does He delay so long? "He [abides] . . . still in the same place" (v. 6), and leaves us pining in sickness, agonizing in pain, bowed down in sorrow, and going forward to mix our tears and our dust in a common grave. We cry like the disciples in the storm to their sleeping Master, "Master, carest thou not that we perish?" (Mark 4:38). To us He does not awake so soon. "O the hope of Israel. . . . why shouldest thou be as a man astonished, as a mighty man that cannot save? yet thou, O Lord, art in the midst of us, and we are called by thy name" (Jer. 14:8-9).

Our very confidence in Christ's ability and willingness to help us thus becomes the occasion of bewildering doubts, and our faith passes through that painful struggle, "Lord, I believe; help thou mine unbelief" (Mark 9:24).

Some of the Reasons for Christ's Delay That May Be Found in This History

We say *"in this history."* Other reasons might be found in the whole divine plan, as it is revealed in the Bible, and others probably there are, outside the Bible and our present life, in the unknown counsels and universe of God. Yet even from this history much may be drawn if we examine it with attention. The works of Christ are all of them mirrors for the history of the world, bringing into a small compass what is permanently and universally true. If the Spirit takes of the things that are Christ's and shows them to us, we may have light on some of the difficult questions that concern our own life and death. We shall try to follow these reasons in the order suggested by the narrative itself.

One reason why Christ delays to interpose against death is,

that *His friends, when dying, may learn confidence in Him and have an opportunity of showing it.* We have no account of the manner of Lazarus's death, and we shall not seek to imagine it. It may have been a joyful one in its expression—or simply peaceful—or silent, as many a good man dies and gives no sign. But the truth remains in all, that death is a great season of instruction to the friends of Christ. Sometimes we can see the process. At other times it is between Him and the soul alone. Sometimes it may be slow, or, again, as rapid as in the lesson He gave on His cross to him who hung beside Him. But we must believe that the period of death has its peculiar use in every spiritual history.

The great end of Christ's dealing with any soul is to convince it that in Him it has an all-sufficient life, and that with Him it can pass safely through every emergency. We have to learn that we are *"complete in him"* (Col. 2:10). We can never learn this in words or by thinking. It must be taught us in the reality of life itself. He takes away from us one thing after another—the friends, the affections, the aims of youth—while He becomes to us a deeper and truer possession. But this course of teaching would want its crown if it did not end in death. Death is the withdrawal of all human supports from around the soul, of its closest affections, of its earth-born vesture and home, of the very body which is its second self—that it may be alone with Christ and feel Him to be enough for it—more to it than every created thing. He invites the soul, and constrains it, to put all its confidence into that last act of surrender—to cast itself, bare of every aid but His, into the mysterious infinite—knowing Him in whom it believes and feeling that underneath it are His everlasting arms. For a man to learn this perfect confidence in Christ, he must die.

On the part of Christ, again, it is the last touch of that purifying fire which He employs to melt the fallen nature—free it from its dross—and fuse it into His own likeness for access to Himself in the heaven of heavens. It is not by any mechanical process that He thus purifies the soul. It can only be by a close spiritual approach to it. But we know something of this manner of dealing with us, even in life. There are supreme moments of experience when we seem to live ages and when all our past history ripens into God's one great lesson for us. Such a moment is that of death, in which Christ matures the soul for the life to come—draws it aside to Himself—presses it, in solitude and secrecy, for a while to His own heart and fulfills His words, "If I go and prepare a place for you, I will come again, and receive you unto myself; that where I am, there ye may be also" (John 14:3).

And yet, sometimes, it is not done so secretly but that the sparkles which fall from the jewel reveal what He is doing for it and where He means to set it. The looks and words of a Christian, when dying, are part of the end for which Christ permits death. It is that dying, as well as living, he may show himself to be the Lord's. To accomplish all this *for* the soul and *through* it, Christ delays His interposition, and the difficulty in the case of Lazarus is not so much that he died, as that he was brought back from the grave to fight life's battle a second time.

Another reason why Christ permits death is, that *the sorrowing friends may learn entire reliance on Him*. It is a subject for study in this chapter how Christ leads on these sisters from a dead brother to the Resurrection and the Life, and teaches them through their loss to gain what they never could lose any more. Had He snatched Lazarus from the brink of death, they would have trembled again at his every sickness. But, when they learn to find their brother in Christ, they are secure of Him forever, and they discover in Christ Himself more than their heart conceived.

Christ separates our friends from us for a while that we may learn to find our all in Himself. He makes their grave the seedbed of immortal hopes, which shall give us back everything that is good in the past, and a joy with it like the joy of harvest. The expression of our resignation in bereavement is as much a triumph of His grace as the calmness He gives to our dying friends. When Martha and Mary can still call Him *"Lord,"* and when their "hope can smile on all other hopes gone from them"—when they can clasp Christ as their portion and desolation around and within—Christ Himself is justified in the permission of death.

Another reason which follows this in the order both of the narrative and of nature is, that, in the midst of death, *the union of sympathy between Christ and his friends is perfected*. Jesus had given many convincing proofs of His love to the household of Bethany while Lazarus lived, but none with that touching tenderness in it which came forth at his grave. The fellowship of suffering brings hearts and lives together more than all the fellowship of joy. There must have been a divine compassion in the Redeemer's look which melted Mary's soul as she fell at His feet and felt that her grief was also His. And when His grief broke out into that trouble of spirit at the grave—when His heart was overpowered by it and *"Jesus wept"* (v. 35)—the mourners knew that He was one with them.

Gethsemane shows us the agony of Christ's soul for man's sin—the grave of Bethany His agony of heart at man's suffering. All that sad, sorrowful walk to the sepulcher where He mingled His tears with theirs, was as necessary to make them feel the sympathy of His soul, as was the great deliverance when He said, "Lazarus, come forth" (John 11:43). Nor need we be at all stumbled by the objection that He could not feel so deeply since He knew what He was about to do. A man may pity the breaking heart of a child although he can see away beyond its short sorrow, and God pities us in the midst of our life's troubles though He perceives the speedy end of them. Be very sure of this, that Christ's grief was as genuine as theirs, and that the compassion of God and of His Son is as true at every step of the road to the grave as it is when it rises up at last into full redemption and the gate of the grave is thrown wide open. To form this fellowship of suffering on the way to death is one reason why Christ permits it. He says, "When thou passest through the waters, I will be with thee" (Isa. 43:2), and we are brought to reply, "[We] went through the flood on foot: there did we rejoice in him" (Ps. 66:6).

Consider this further, that it is by delaying to interpose against death that *God makes this a world of spiritual probation.* When He abode in the same place and lingered on His way to Bethany, Christ tried the character, not only of the sisters, but of all who knew the case. Superficiality fell away—secret unbelief broke out into scorn—and those alone stood the test whose souls had sought and found in Him what the soul needs. Christ's delays are the touchstones of spiritual life.

You who would have Him never suffer the tears of His people

to fall—who would wish Him to heal His friends so soon as they are sick—or raise them to life the instant that they die—reflect on what you ask. You would lead men to seek Him, not from the love they bear Himself, but from their desire for His outward benefits. You would create, in your impatience, a world of formalism and hypocrisy—the very world which God disproved in the face of Satan when He said, "Doth Job fear God for nought?" (Job 1:9). But God defers the time for interposition—makes all things outwardly come alike to all—and causes calamity and death to visit with an impartial step the homes of His friends—in order that He may sift men's characters and prepare them for the day of judgment. Those who would have Christ interpose immediately against death mistake entirely the structure of the world we are placed in. To be consistent, they should go back and remonstrate against the creation of responsible agents, and the possibility of sin that flows from it. Death is the consequence of these things, and it is at the same time a veil let down over the face of God's throne, to hide spiritual things from the eye of sense, and to make faith the instrument of the soul's recovery and training. Death cannot be abolished until the history of this world is completed.

We mention, as a last reason for Christ's delay to interpose against death, that *He brings in thereby a grander final issue*. Had He come and arrested this sickness midway, or raised Lazarus to life so soon as he died, the gladness of the friends would not have been so great, nor would His own triumph over death have been so illustrious. But He patiently waits His hour, while the mourners weep and the scoffers scorn. Men must interpose when they can, but the Son of God interposes when He wills. The wisdom with which He chooses His time makes His delay not callous nor cruel, but considerate of our best interests in withholding for a while that He may bless us at last with an overflowing hand. Could the mourners see it as He does, they would willingly acquiesce, and would go forth patiently sowing in tears that they might have a more abundant reaping-time of joy.

It is in this interval of delay that our life is cast. The world is represented by this home of Bethany before Christ reached the grave, and all the phases of character, and all the stages of Christ's progressive advance may be seen in the hearts of men around us. But at whatever step of His journey, man's faith may discern Him, He is surely on His way. The tide of eternal life is setting in toward the world of graves, and its swell and its murmur can be already perceived by all who have a soul to feel the heaving of Christ's heart. Amid the tears and sobs of the bereaved friends, whose sorrows still touch Him, He is moving to the sepulcher. His presence, though unseen, can be heard and felt in whispered consolations—in the faith and hope which His Spirit infuses into the soul. Those who know Him for what He is recognize a Friend who weeps in sympathy with them, and who walks by their side to the tomb which His voice shall yet open. The delay seems long, but He counts the hours as we do, and not for a single one will He linger beyond what infinite wisdom sees fit. One result of this delay shall be a grander final issue. He permits His friends to descend with broken ranks into the swellings of Jordan, but He will lead them forth on the other side in one fully-marshaled and bannered host. He puts the jewels one by one into His crown within the secret of His palace, that He may bring them out at last, resplendent and complete as a royal diadem, from the hand of His God. Patient waiting shall have its full compensation on that day, and divine delay justifies itself before the universe in glorious and everlasting results. Could we see to the end, it would reconcile us even now. He discerns it for us and withholds His hand from premature and imperfect interference. After their burst of weeping, He hushes the separate voices for a season in the silence of death, until they can awake and sing in full harmony, that their united praise may still the enemy and the avenger, and be His glory and their own joy forever.

One thing connected with all these reasons and impressed upon us by the present narrative cannot be omitted, that *there is a fitness in Christ being absent from the world while death reigns.* Mary felt this, "Lord, if thou hadst been here, my brother had not died." Christ could not be present and see death strike down His friends without interposing. We never read that this enemy of man was permitted to exercise his power before the open face of the Son of God. It would be inconsistent with the honor of Him who is the Lord of life. And therefore Christ must be absent from the world while death and the grave maintain their sway. This is befitting His dignity, and it furnishes one reason more why we should desire the appearing of that blessed and gracious face before which death and every shadow shall flee away. Meantime He gathers the fold of His cloud over His countenance, that we may not think He looks with cold indifference on our anguish, until He shall withdraw the veil fully and forever. Happy those to whose eye of faith the cloud is already pierced, and who feel in the heart that sunshine of His face which shall give life and light at last to all the dead in Christ.

What a miserable earth would it be without this hope, without this possession!—the desolate home of Bethany without the great Friend—men dying, mourners weeping, graves filling up, and death reigning forever! Why then should a world exist to pass through ceaseless anguish to such a close—to be a wide eternal burying-ground, where tears are only dried on the cheek by death, but never wiped away by the hand of God? How should our hearts leap up with exulting joy to think that there is a Christ, and how should we thank Him, as we alone can, by accepting Him as God's unspeakable gift! There is a way of being certain of this blessed hope, by having Him now in the soul as its life. If we are quickened from the death of trespasses and sins, and raised up to sit with Him even now in heavenly places, we know that He can and will redeem us from the power of the grave. There must be a world in reserve for such a divine life. It will no more be an incredible thing with us that God should raise the dead. And now, on the way, the great Lord and Giver of life is pressing on you His gracious offer, without which immortality has no ray of clearness or of joy. Jesus said, "I am the resurrection, and the life: he that believeth in me, though he were dead, yet shall he live: and whosoever liveth and believeth in me shall never die! Believest thou this?" (John 11:25–26). See that you refuse not Him that speaks, and rest not until with all your heart you can reply, "Yea, Lord: I believe that thou art the Christ, the Son of God, which should come into the world" (v. 27).

Death of Stephen

Robert Murray McCheyne (1813–1843) is one of the brightest lights of the Church of Scotland. Born in Edinburgh, he was educated in Edinburgh and licensed to preach in 1835. For a brief time, he assisted his friend Andrew A. Bonar at Larbert and Duniplace. In 1836 he was ordained and installed as pastor of Saint Peter's Church, Dundee, where he served until his untimely death two months short of his thirtieth birthday. He was known for his personal sanctity and his penetrating ministry of the Word, and great crowds came to hear him preach. *The Memoirs of and Remains of Robert Murray McCheyne,* by Andrew Bonar, is a Christian classic that every minister of the gospel should read.

This sermon, preached August 13, 1837, was taken from *The Additional Remains of the Rev. Robert Murray McCheyne,* published in Edinburgh by William Oliphant in 1846.

7

Death of Stephen

And they stoned Stephen, calling upon God, and saying, Lord Jesus, receive my spirit. (Acts 7:59)

STEPHEN WAS THE FIRST to die as a martyr in the cause of Christ. He seems to have resembled the Savior more than any that followed after. His very face appeared like the face of an angel. His irresistible wisdom in arguing with the Jews was very like Christ. His praying for his enemies with his dying breath nearly in the same words as the Savior and his recommending his soul into the hands of the Lord Jesus were in the same spirit of confidence as that in which Christ said: "Father, into thy hands I commend my spirit" (Luke 23:46). There cannot be a doubt that it was by looking to Jesus that he became thus Christlike. The last view which he got of Christ seems especially to have given him that heavenly composure in dying, which is so much above nature.

Two things are to be noticed: (1) That it was a sight of Christ at the right hand of God; and (2) that it was a sight of Christ standing there. Christ being at the right hand of God is mentioned sixteen times in the Bible. Thirteen times He is described as seated there, twice as being there; but here only is He spoken of as standing. This appears to have made a deep and lively impression on the mind of Stephen, for he cries out: "Behold, I see the heavens opened, and the Son of man standing on the right hand of God" (Acts 7:56). Then, with a sweet assurance that Christ's hands were stretched out to receive him, he cried: "Lord Jesus, receive my spirit."

Doctrine: Since Christ is at the right hand of God, and since He rises up to receive the dying believer, believers should commend their spirit to the Lord Jesus.

The Believer's Sins Must Be Pardoned

If Christ be at the right hand of God, the believer's sins must be pardoned so that he can peacefully say: "Lord Jesus, receive my spirit." If the grave had closed over the head of Christ forever—if the stone had remained at the mouth of the sepulcher to this day—then we might well be in doubt whether He had suffered enough in the stead of sinners. "If Christ be not risen . . . your faith is also vain. . . . ye are yet in your sins" (1 Cor. 15:14–17). But is it true that Christ is at the right hand of God? Then the stone has been rolled away from the sepulcher. God has let Him go free from the curse that was laid on Him. The justice of God is quite satisfied. If you saw a criminal put into prison and the prison doors closed behind him, and if you never saw him come out again, then you might well believe that he was still lying in prison and still enduring the just sentence of the law. But if you saw the prison doors fly open and the prisoner going free—if you saw him walking at large in the streets—then you would know at once that he had satisfied the justice of his country. You would know that he had suffered all that it was needful to suffer and that he had paid the uttermost farthing.

So with the Lord Jesus. He was counted a criminal—the crimes of guilty sinners against God were all laid at His door, and He was condemned on account of them. He was hurried away to the death of the cross, and the gloomy prison house of His rocky sepulcher—the stone was rolled to the mouth of the grave. If you never saw Him come out, then you might well believe that He was still enduring the just sentence of the law. But, lo! "he is risen; he is not here" (Mark 16:6). "The Lord is risen indeed" (Luke 24:34). God, who was His judge, has raised Him from the dead and set Him at His own right hand in the heavenly places, so that you may be quite sure He has satisfied the justice of God. He has suffered everything that it was needful for Him to suffer. He has paid the uttermost farthing. Now, is there any of you hearing me who cleaves to the Lord Jesus? Is this the Savior whom you take to be your surety? "Be of good cheer; thy sins be forgiven thee" (Matt. 9:2). For if your surety is free, then you are free. It was this that gave such a tranquil peace to the dying Stephen. He had the same vile nature that you have. He had committed the same sins as you. He had the same condemnation over him. But when he saw Jesus Christ, whom he had taken as his surety, standing free at the right hand of God, then he felt that the condemnation had been already borne—that God's anger was quite turned away front his soul. Thus being inwardly persuaded of pardon, he committed his spirit into the hand of Christ: "Lord Jesus, receive my spirit."

Oh! friends, cleave to the same Lord Jesus. He is still as free as He was when Stephen died. He always will be free. Death has no more power over Him, for He has suffered all. Take Him as your surety. Cleave to Him as your Savior, and you may this day have the same peace that Stephen had and may die with the same peaceful breast, saying: "Lord Jesus, receive my spirit."

The Believer Is Accepted with God

If Christ be at the right hand of God, then the believer is accepted with God, and may peacefully say with Stephen: "Lord Jesus, receive my spirit."

The Son of God came to be a surety for men in two respects: (1) In suffering the wrath which they deserved to suffer; and (2) in rendering the obedience which men had neglected to render. If He stood as surety in suffering, then every dying sinner that cleaved to Him was to be freed from the curse of God. If He stood as surety in obeying, then He and every sinner that cleaved to Him was to be rewarded with a place in glory. Now, if Christ had not risen from the dead, then it would have been manifest that God had not accepted His obedience as worthy of eternal life. But if Christ is risen, and not only so, but if He be at the right hand of God, the place of highest glory in heaven where are pleasures forevermore, then I am quite sure that God is satisfied with Christ as a surety for man. If you saw some peer of the realm sent away by the king upon a distant and hazardous undertaking with the promise that, if he succeeded, he should be advanced to the seat nearest the throne—if you never saw that peer return to claim his reward, then you would say at once that he had failed in his undertaking. But if you saw him return and the applause of assembled multitudes, and if you saw him received into the palace of the king and seated on the right hand of majesty, then you would say at once that he had succeeded in that which he undertook. You would say that the king upon the throne was well pleased with him for it.

Just so, if you had been in heaven on that most wonderful day that ever was, of which the Christian Sabbath is an ever-enduring monument, when Christ ascended to His Father and our Father—had you seen the smile of ineffable complacency wherewith God received back into glory the surety of men, saying: "Thou art my Son, this day have I begotten thee" (Ps. 2:7; Acts 13:33); as if He said: "Never until this day did I see thee so worthy to he called my Son"; and again: "Sit thou at my right hand, until I make thine enemies thy footstool" (Ps. 110:1; Matt. 22:44; Mark 12:36; Luke 20:43)—had you seen all this, then you would have known how excellent the obedience of Christ is in the eyes of the Father. But all this obedience was endured, not for Himself; but as a surety for men. He was accepted Himself before He left heaven. He was infinitely near and dear to the Father and did not need to become man to obey for Himself. Everything that Jesus Christ did or suffered was as a surety in the stead of sinners. Do you take Him for your surety? Do you cleave to the Lord Jesus, because you have nothing of your own to recommend you to God? Then look up with the eye of faith and see Him at the right hand of God. If you cleave to Him, you are as much accepted with God as Christ is. You are as near to God as your surety is. Ah! it was this that gave the dying Stephen such calm tranquillity. He had the same vile nature that you have. He had as little obedience to God as you have. He was a naked sinner, as you are. But he took the Lord Jesus to be his surety—the man in his stead. So that, when he saw Him at the right hand of God, he felt that Christ was accepted and that he, also, was accepted in the Beloved. And thus, being inwardly persuaded that in Christ he had a safe way to the Father, he cried, with dying breath: "Lord Jesus, receive my spirit."

Oh! trembling, naked sinner, cleave to the Lord Jesus. He is as much offered to you as He was to Stephen. Take Him as your surety. Cleave to Him as your Savior, and you may this day have the same sense of acceptance which Stephen had. You may die with the same sweetly confiding cry: "Lord Jesus, receive my spirit."

The Believer Is Given Great Confidence

If Christ stands up to receive the dying believer, this gives the believer great confidence, so that he may peacefully say: "Lord Jesus, receive my spirit."

When believing souls seek for peace and joy in believing, they do very generally confine their view to Christ upon the earth. They remember Him as the good Shepherd seeking the lost sheep. They look to Him sitting by the well of Samaria. They remember Him saying to the sick of the palsy: "Be of good cheer; thy sins be forgiven thee." But they too seldom think of looking where Stephen looked—to where Jesus is now—at the right hand of God. Now, my friends, remember, if you would be whole Christians, you must look to a whole Christ. You must lift your eye from the cross to the throne, and you will find Him the same Savior in all—"the same yesterday, and to day, and for ever" (Heb. 13:8). I have already observed, that wherever Christ is mentioned as being at the right hand of God, He is spoken of as seated there upon His throne. Here, and here only, are we told that He is standing. In other places He is described as enjoying His glory and entered into His rest. But here He is described as risen from His throne and standing at the right hand of God.

He rises to intercede: "He is able also to save to the uttermost that come unto God by him, seeing he ever liveth to make intercession for them" (Heb. 7:25). How often would a believer be a castaway if it were not for the great Intercessor! How often faith fails! "Flesh and heart faint and fail." But see here, Christ never fails. On the deathbed, often the mind is taken off the Savior by pains of body and distress of mind. But, oh! happy soul that has truly accepted Christ. See here, He rises from His throne to pray for you when you cannot pray for yourself. Look up to Him with the eye of faith and cry: "Lord Jesus, receive my spirit."

He rises to defend. The world is a sore enemy to the believer—by temptation on the one hand and persecution on the other. Oh! how hard it strives to cast him down. Happy believer, you are safe in a dying hour! First, because the world cannot reach beyond death. The sneering tongue cannot spit its venom beyond the grave. The stone of violence may kill the body, but it has no more that it can do. Second, even if it were possible that some arrow of the world might reach beyond the grave, Jesus has risen up to defend. His everlasting arms are underneath the departing soul.

The devil is a worse enemy in that hour. He stands close by the dying bed. He often molests, but he cannot destroy, if you are cleaving to Jesus. Christ has all power in heaven and in earth, and He rises up to defend your soul. "It is I," he says, "be not afraid" (Matt. 14:27; Mark 6:50; John 6:20). Ah! dear friends, cleave to the Lord Jesus now if you would have Him to stand up for you in a dying hour—if you would cry with confidence: "Lord Jesus, receive my spirit."

He rises to receive the departing soul. This is the sweetest of all comforts to the godly. It is a sweet thought that the holy angels are waiting to receive the believing soul. When Lazarus died, the good angels carried him into Abraham's bosom. But, oh! it is sweeter far, to think that Jesus looks down upon the dying bed and stands up to receive the soul that loves Him.

Oh! dear brethren, He is the same kind Savior in death that He is through life. Once you lived without prayer—without God—without Christ in the world. Did Christ not stretch out the hands all the day, even then? Once you were lying under convictions of sin. You felt yourself worthy of hell and that God would be just if He never had mercy on your soul. Did not Christ draw near to your soul, saying: "Peace be unto you?" (Luke 24:36; John 20:19, 21, 26). Again, you were groaning under the power of temptation, crying against indwelling sin: "O wretched man! who shall deliver me from the body of this death?" Did not Christ draw near and say: "My grace is sufficient for thee: for my strength is made perfect in weakness" (2 Cor. 12:9)? Once more, you may yet groan under the weight of dying agonies. The last enemy is death. It may be a hard struggle; it may be a dark valley. Yet look where Stephen looked.

Lo! Jesus is standing at the right hand of God, waiting to receive you to Himself. Oh! sweet death, when God is with you, the Spirit within you, and Christ waiting to receive you. Behold! He stretches out His hands to receive your departing spirit. Breathe it into His hand, saying: "Lord Jesus, receive my spirit."

Conclusion

Learn that death is no death to the Christian: "Whosoever liveth and believeth in me shall never die" (John 11:26). It is only giving the soul into the hand of Christ. He knows its value, for He died for it.

Learn that to die is, to the believer, better than to live. If Christ rises up to receive the soul, then the soul goes to be with Jesus. But to be with Christ is to be in glory; therefore, it is far better. Oh! be willing, Christians, to be absent from the body and present with the Lord. There you shall be free from pain of persecuting stones—no more sneering, cruel friends; no more doubts about your soul; no more sin within your heart. *"Oh, that I had the wings of a dove, that I might flee away and be at rest!"*

Learn the dreadfulness of having no interest in Jesus Christ. You must die. Yet how will you die, poor Christless soul? To whom will you commend your dying spirit? There will be no good angels waiting around your bed—no gentle hands of ministering spirits stretched out to receive your trembling soul. You will have no Christ rising up to receive you. You never washed in His blood—you would not come to Him to have life. He often stretched out His hands, but you pushed them away. Now He will have no pity for you. You will have no God—God will not be your God—He will not be your friend. You have always been His enemy. Your proud heart would not be reconciled to Him. Now you will find Him an enemy indeed.

Where will you go? Die you must. Your breath must cease. These eyes that look on me this day must close in death. That heart which you feel beating in your bosom must cease to beat. And what will you do within your soul? To whom will you commend it—a naked, guilty, shivering thing, with the wrath of God abiding on it? None of the angels will dare to shelter it. No rocks or caves or mountains can hide it. Hell itself will not be a hiding place from the just wrath of God. Oh! be wise now: "Turn ye, turn ye . . . why will ye die?" (Ezek. 33:11).

Learn, if you have lost any friends in Christ, to be comforted over them. It is true they are gone from you, but remember they have gone into far tenderer hands. You stood up to bend over their dying body; but the Lord Jesus stood up to receive their undying soul. Your feeble but affectionate hands were stretched out to smooth their dying pillow, but the almighty hands of the Savior formed a sweeter, softer bed for their departing soul. Follow their faith. Look to the same Savior and when you come to die, you will use with your heart or with your tongue the same sweet words: "Lord Jesus, receive my spirit."

NOTES

Victory Over Death

Frederick W. Robertson (1816-1853) wanted to be a soldier, but he yielded to his father's decision that he take orders in the Anglican church. The courage that he would have shown on the battlefield, he displayed in the pulpit, where he fearlessly declared truth as he saw it. Never strong physically, he experienced deep depression; he questioned his faith, and he often wondered if his ministry was doing any good. He died a young man, in great pain, but in great faith and courage. He had ministered for only six years at Trinity Chapel, Brighton, but today his printed sermons have taken his brave message around the world.

This sermon was taken from his *Sermons, Third Series,* published in 1900 in London by Kegan Paul, Trench, Trubner and Company.

FREDERICK W. ROBERTSON

8

Victory Over Death

The sting of death is sin; and the strength of sin is the law. But thanks be to God, which giveth us the victory through our Lord Jesus Christ. (1 Corinthians 15:56–57)

ON SUNDAY LAST I endeavored to bring before you the subject of that which Scripture calls the glorious liberty of the Sons of God. The two points on which we were trying to get clear notions were these: what is meant by being under the law, and what is meant by being free from the law? When the Bible says that a man led by the Spirit is not under the law, it does not mean that he is free because he may sin without being punished for it, but it means that he is free because being taught by God's Spirit to love what His law commands he is no longer conscious of acting from restraint. The law does not drive him because the Spirit leads him.

There is a state when we recognize God but do not love God in Christ. It is that state when we admire what is excellent but are not able to perform it. It is a state when the love of good comes to nothing, dying away in a mere desire. That is the state of nature, when we are under the law and not converted to the love of Christ. And then there is another state, when God writes His law upon our hearts by love instead of fear. The one state is this, "Ye cannot do the things that ye would" (Gal. 5:17). The other state is this, "I will walk at liberty; for I seek thy precepts" (Ps. 119:45).

Just so far therefore, as a Christian is led by the Spirit, he is a conqueror. A Christian in full possession of his privileges is a man whose very step ought to have in it all the elasticity of triumph, and whose very look ought to have in it all the brightness of victory. And just so far as a Christian suffers sin to struggle in him and overcome his resolutions, just so far he is under the law. And that is the key to the whole doctrine of the New Testament. From first to last the great truth put forward is: the law can neither save you nor sanctify you. The gospel can do both, for it is rightly and emphatically called the perfect law of liberty.

We proceed today to a further illustration of this subject of Christian victory. In the verses that I have read out, the apostle has evidently the same subject in his mind: slavery through the law; victory through the gospel. "The strength of sin," he says, "is the law." God gives us the victory through Christ. And when we are familiar with St. Paul's trains of thinking, we find this idea coming in perpetually. It runs like a colored thread through embroidery, appearing on the upper surface every now and then in a different shape—a leaf, it may be, or a flower but the same thread still, if you only trace it back with your finger. And this was the golden recurring thread in the mind of Paul. Restraint and law cannot check sin. They only gall it and make it struggle and rebel. The love of God in Christ, that, and only that can give man the victory.

But in this passage the idea of victory is brought to bear upon the most terrible of all a Christian's enemies. It is faith here conquering in death. And the apostle brings together all the believer's antagonists—the law's power, sin, and death, the chief antagonist of all. Then, as it were on a conqueror's battlefield, shouts over them the hymn of triumph: "Thanks be to God, which giveth us the victory, through our Lord Jesus Christ." We shall take up these two points to dwell upon: (1) the awfulness that hangs around the dying hour, and (2) faith conquering in death.

The Awfulness That Hangs Around the Dying Hour

That which makes it peculiarly terrible to die is asserted in this passage to be, guilt. We lay a stress upon this expression—

the sting. It is not said that sin is the only bitt⟨...⟩ the sting which contains in it the venom of ⟨...⟩ torture. And in truth brethren, it is no mark of ⟨...⟩ lightly of human dying. We may do it in bravado or in w⟨...⟩ness, but no man who thinks can call it a trifling thing to die. True thoughtfulness must shrink from death without Christ. There is a world of untold sensations crowded into that moment, when a man puts his hand to his forehead and feels the damp upon it which tells him his hour is come. He has been waiting for death all his life, and now it is come. It is all over. His chance is past, and his eternity is settled. None of us know, except by guess, what that sensation is. Myriads of human beings have felt it to whom life was dear, but they never spoke out their feelings, for such things are untold. And to every individual man throughout all eternity that sensation in its fullness can come but once. It is mockery for a man to speak lightly of that which he cannot know until it comes.

Now the first cause that makes it a solemn thing to die is the instinctive cleaving of everything that lives to its own existence. That unutterable thing which we call our being—the idea of parting with it is agony. It is the first and the intensest desire of living things to be. Enjoyment, blessedness, everything we long for, is wrapped up in being. Darkness, and all that the spirit recoils from, is contained in this idea not to be. It is in virtue of this unquenchable impulse that the world, in spite of all the misery that is in it, continues to struggle on. What are war and trade and labor and professions? Are they all the result of struggling to be great? No, they are the result of struggling *to be*. The first thing that men and nations labor for is existence. Reduce the nation or the man to their last resources, and only see what marvelous energy of contrivance the love of being arms them with. Read back the pauper's history at the end of seventy years—his strange sad history, in which scarcely a single day could ensure subsistence for the morrow—and yet learn what he has done these long years in the stern struggle with impossibility to hold his being where everything is against him, and to keep an existence, whose only conceivable charm is this, that it *is* existence.

Now it is with this intense passion for being that the idea of eath clashes. Let us search why it is we shrink from death. This reason, we shall find, that it presents to us the idea of *not being*. Talk as we will of immortality, there is an obstinate feeling that we cannot master, that we end in death, and *that* may be felt together with the firmest belief of a resurrection. Our faith tells us one thing, and our sensations tell us another. When we die, we are surrendering in truth all that with which we have associated existence. All that we know of life is connected with a shape, a form, a body of materialism. Now that that is palpably melting away into nothingness, the boldest heart may be excused a shudder, when there is forced upon it, in spite of itself, the idea of ceasing forever.

The second reason is not one of imagination at all, but most sober reality. It is a solemn thing to die because it is the parting with all around which the heart's best affections have twined themselves. There are some men who have not the capacity for keen enjoyment. Their affections have nothing in them of intensity, and so they pass through life without ever so uniting themselves with what they meet, that there would be anything of pain in the severance. Of course, with them the bitterness of death does not attach so much to the idea of parting. But how is it with human nature generally? Our feelings do not weaken as we go on in life. Emotions are less shown, and we get a command over our features and our expressions. But the man's feelings are deeper than the boy's. It is length of time that makes attachment. We become wedded to the sights and sounds of this lovely world more closely as years go on.

Young men, with nothing rooted deep, are prodigal of life. It is an adventure to them, rather than a misfortune, to leave their country forever. With the old man it is like tearing his own heart from him. And so it was that when Lot quitted Sodom, the younger members of his family went on gladly. It is a touching truth. It was the aged one who looked behind to the home which had so many recollections connected with it. And, therefore, it is that when men approach that period of existence when they must go, there is an instinctive lingering over things that they shall never see again. Every time the sun sets, every time the old man sees his children gathering around him, there is a filling of the eye with an emotion that we can understand. There is upon his soul the thought of parting, that strange wrench from all we love that makes death (say what moralists will of it) a bitter thing.

Another pang that belongs to death we find in the sensation of loneliness which attaches to it. Have we ever seen a ship preparing to sail with its load of pauper emigrants to a distant colony? If we have we know what that desolation is which comes from feeling unfriended on a new and untried excursion. All beyond the seas, to the ignorant poor man, is a strange land. They are going away from the helps and the friendships and the companionships of life, scarcely knowing what is before them. And it is in such a moment, when a man stands upon a deck taking his last look of his fatherland, that there comes upon him a sensation new, strange, and inexpressibly miserable—the feeling of being alone in the world.

With all the bitterness of such a moment, it is but a feeble image when placed by the side of the loneliness of death. We die alone. We go on our dark mysterious journey for the first time in all our existence without one to accompany us. Friends are beside our bed; they must stay behind. Grant that a Christian has something like familiarity with the Most High, that breaks this solitary feeling. But what is it with the mass of men? It is a question full of loneliness to them. What is it they are to see? What are they to meet? Is it not true, that, to the larger number of this congregation, there is no one point in all eternity on which the eye can fix distinctly and rest gladly—nothing beyond the grave, except a dark space into which they must plunge alone?

And yet, with all these ideas no doubt vividly before his mind, it was none of them that the apostle selected as the crowning bitterness of dying. It was not the thought of surrendering existence. It was not the parting from all bright and lovely things. It was not the shudder of sinking into the sepulcher alone. "The sting of death is *sin*."

Now there are two ways in which this deep truth applies itself. There is something that appalls in death when there are distinct separate acts of guilt resting on the memory. There is something too in the possession of a guilty heart, which is quite another thing from acts of sin, that makes it an awful thing to die. There are some who carry about with them the dreadful secret of sin that has been done; guilt that has a name. A man has injured someone. He has made money or gotten on by unfair means. He has been unchaste. He has done some of those thousand things of life which leave upon the heart the dark spot that will not come out. All these are sins that you can count up and number. And the recollection of things like these is that agony which we call remorse. Many of us have remembrances of this kind which are fatal to serenity. We shut them out, but it will not do. They bide their time, and then suddenly present themselves together with the thought of a judgment seat. When a guilty man begins to think of dying, it is like a vision of the Son of Man presenting itself and calling out the voices of all the unclean spirits in the man, "Art thou come hither to torment us before the time?" (Matt. 8:29).

But it is a mistake if we suppose that is the common way in which sin stings at the thought of death. Men who have lived the career of passionate life have distinct and accumulated acts of guilt before their eyes. But with most men it is not guilty acts, but guiltiness of heart that weighs the heaviest. Only take yesterday as a specimen of life. What was it with most of us? A day of sin. Was it sin palpable and dark, such as we shall remember painfully this day year? No, my friends, unkindness, petulance, wasted time, opportunities lost, frivolous conversation, *that* was our chief guilt. And yet with all that trifling as it may be, when it comes to be the history of life, does it not leave behind a restless undefinable sense of fault, a vague idea of debt, but to what extent we know not, perhaps the more wretched just because it is uncertain?

My Christian friends, this is the sting of sinfulness, the wretched consciousness of an unclean heart. It is just this feeling, "God is not my friend. I am going on to the grave, and no *man* can say anything against me. But my heart is not right. I want a river like that which the ancients fabled—the river of forgetfulness—that I might go down into it and bathe and come up a new man. It is not so much what I have done; it is what I am. Who shall save me from myself?" Oh, it is a desolate thing to think of the coffin when that thought is in all its misery before the soul. It is the sting of death.

And now let us bear one thing in mind, the sting of sin is not a constant pressure. It may be that we live many years in the world before a death in our own family forces the thought personally home. Many years before all those sensations that are so often the precursors of the tomb—the quick short cough, lassitude, emaciation, pain—come in startling suddenness upon us in our young vigor, and make us feel what it is to be here with death inevitable to ourselves. And when those things become habitual, habit makes delicacy the same forgetful thing as health, so that neither in sickness, nor in health, is the thought of death a constant pressure. It is only now and then. But so often as death is a reality, the sting of death is sin.

Once more we remark, that all this power of sin to agonize is traced by the apostle to the law—"the strength of sin is the law." By that he means to say that sin would not be so violent if it were not for the attempt of God's law to restrain it. It is the law which makes sin strong. And he does not mean particularly the law of Moses. He means any law and all law. Law is what forbids and threatens. Law bears gallingly on those who want to break it. And St. Paul declares this, that no law, not even God's law, can make men righteous in heart, unless the Spirit has taught men's hearts to acquiesce in the law. It can only force out into rebellion the sin that is in them.

It is so with a nation's law. The voice of the nation must go along with it. It must be the expression of their own feeling, and then they will have it obeyed. But if it is only the law of a government, a law which is against the whole spirit of the people, there is first the murmur of a nation's disapprobation, and then there is transgression, and then, if the law be vindicated with a high hand, the next step is the bursting that law asunder in national revolution. And so it is with God's law. It will never control a man long who does not from his heart love it. First comes a sensation of restraint, and then comes a murmuring of the heart; and last, there comes the rising of a passion in its giant might, made desperate by restraint. That is the law giving strength to sin.

And, therefore, if all we know of God be this, that He has made laws and that it is terrible to break them; if all our idea of religion be this, that it is a thing of commands and hindrances—

thou shalt, and thou shalt not—we are under the law and there is no help for it. We *must* shrink from the encounter with death.

Faith Conquering in Death

And, before we enter upon this topic, there are two general remarks that we have to make. The first is, the elevating power of faith. There is nothing in all this world that ever led man on to real victory but faith. Faith is that looking forward to a future with something like certainty that raises man above the narrow feelings of the present. Even in this life he is a greater man, a man of more elevated character, who is steadily pursuing a plan that requires some years to accomplish than he who is living by the day. Look forward but ten years and plan for it, live for it. There is something of manhood, something of courage required to conquer the thousand things that stand in your way. And therefore it is, that faith, and nothing but faith, gives victory in death. It is that elevation of character which we get from looking steadily and forever forward, until eternity becomes a real home to us, that enables us to look down upon the last struggle and the funeral and the grave, not as the great end of all, but only as something that stands between us and the end. We are conquerors of death when we are able to look beyond it.

Our second remark is for the purpose of fixing special attention upon this, that ours is not merely to be victory, it is to be victory through Christ. "Thanks be to God which giveth us the victory through our Lord Jesus Christ." Victory, mere victory, over death is no unearthly thing. You may get it by infidelity. Only let a man sin long enough, and desperately enough to shut judgment altogether out of his creed, and then you have a man who can bid defiance to the grave. It was so that our country's greatest infidel historian met death. He quitted the world without parade and without display. If we want a specimen of victory apart from Christ, we have it on his deathbed. He left all this strange world of restlessness, calmly, like an unreal show that must go to pieces, and he himself an unreality departing from it. A skeptic can be a conqueror in death.

Or again, mere manhood may give us a victory. He who has only learned not to be afraid to die, has not learned much. We have steel and nerve enough in our hearts to dare anything. And after all, it is a triumph so common as scarcely to deserve the name. Felons die on the scaffold like men; soldiers can be hired by tens of thousands, for a few pence a day, to front death in its worst form. Every minute that we live sixty of the human race are passing away, and the greater part with courage—the weak and the timid, as well as the resolute. Courage is a very different thing from the Christian's victory.

Once more, necessity can make man conqueror over death. We can make up our minds to anything when it once becomes inevitable. It is the agony of suspense that makes danger dreadful. History can tell us that men can look with desperate calmness upon hell itself when once it has become a certainty. And it is this after all, that commonly makes the dying hour so quiet a thing. It is more dreadful in the distance than in the reality. When a man feels that there is no help and he must go, he lays him down to die as quietly as a tired traveler wraps himself in his cloak to sleep. It is quite another thing from all this that Paul meant by victory.

In the first place, it is the prerogative of a Christian to be conqueror over doubt. Do we all know what doubt means? Perchance not. There are some men who have never believed enough to doubt. There are some who have never thrown their hopes within such earnestness on the world to come as to feel anxiety for fear it would not all be true. But every one who knows what faith is knows, too, what is the desolation of doubt. We pray until we begin to ask, Is there one who hears, or am I whispering to myself? We hear the consolation administered to the bereaved, and we see the coffin lowered into the grave, and the thought comes, What if all this doctrine of a life to come be but the dream of man's imaginative mind, carried on from age to age and so believed because it is a venerable superstition? Now Christ gives us victory over that terrible suspicion in two ways. First, He does it by His own resurrection. We have a fact there that all the metaphysics about impossibility cannot rob us. In moments of perplexity we look back to this. The grave has once, and more than once, at the Redeemer's bidding, given up its dead. It is a world fact. It tells us what the Bible means by our resurrection—not a spiritual rising into new holiness merely—that, but also something more. It means that in our own proper identity, we shall live again. Make that thought real, and God has given you, so far, victory over the grave through Christ.

There is another way in which we get the victory over doubt, and that is by living in Christ. All doubt comes from living out of habits of affectionate obedience to God. By idleness, by neglected power, we lose our power of realizing things not seen. Let a man be religious and irreligious at intervals—irregular, inconsistent, without some distinct thing to live for—it is a matter of impossibility that he can be free from doubts. He must make up his mind for a dark life. Doubts can only be dispelled by that kind of active life that realizes Christ. And there is no faith that gives a victory so steadily triumphant as that. When such a man comes near the opening of the vault, it is no world of sorrows he is entering upon. He is only going to see things that he has felt, for he has been living in heaven. He has his grasp on things that other men are only groping after and touching now and then. Live above this world and there the powers of the world to come are so upon you that there is no room for doubt.

Besides all this, it is a Christian's privilege to have victory over the fear of death. And here it is exceedingly easy to paint what after all is only the image-picture of a dying hour. It is the easiest thing to represent the dying Christian as a man who always sinks into the grave full of hope, full of triumph, in the certain hope of a blessed resurrection. Friends, we must paint things in the sober colors of truth—not as they might be supposed to be, but as they are. Often that is only a picture. Either very few deathbeds are Christian ones or else triumph is a very different thing from what the word generally implies. Solemn, subdued, full of awe and full of solemnity, is the dying hour generally of the holiest men, sometimes almost darkness. Rapture is a rare thing, except in books and scenes.

Let us understand what really is the victory over fear. It may be rapture or it may not. All that depends very much on temperament. After all, the broken words of a dying man are a very poor index of his real state before God. Rapturous hope has been granted to martyrs in peculiar moments. It is on record of a minister of our own church that his expectation of seeing God in Christ became so intense as his last hour drew near that his physician was compelled to bid him calm his transports, because in so excited a state he could not die. A strange unnatural energy was imparted to his muscular frame by his nerves overstrung with triumph. But it fosters a dangerous feeling to take cases like those as precedents. It leads to that most terrible of all unrealities—the acting of a deathbed scene. A Christian conqueror dies calmly. Brave men in battle do not boast that they are not afraid. Courage is so natural to them that they are not conscious they are doing anything out of the common way—Christian bravery is a deep, calm thing, unconscious of itself. There are more triumphant deathbeds than we count, if we only remember this—true fearlessness makes no parade.

Oh, it is not only in those passionate effusions in which the ancient martyrs spoke sometimes of panting for the crushing of their limbs by the lions in the amphitheater, or of holding out their arms to embrace the flames that were to curl around them—it is not then only that Christ has stood by His servants and made them more than conquerors. There may be something of earthly excitement in all that. Every day His servants are dying modestly and peacefully—not a word of victory on their lips, but Christ's deep triumph in their hearts—watching the slow progress of their own decay, and yet so far emancipated from personal anxiety that they are still able to think and to plan for others, not knowing that they are doing any great thing. They die and the world hears nothing of them. Yet theirs was the completest victory. They came to the battlefield, the field to which they had been looking forward all their lives, and the enemy was not to be found. There was no foe to fight with.

The last form in which a Christian gets the victory over death is by means of his resurrection. It seems to have been this which was chiefly alluded to by the apostle here, for he says, "When this corruptible shall have put on incorruption . . . *then* shall be brought to pass the saying which is written, Death is swallowed up in victory" (1 Cor. 15:54). And to say the truth, friends, it is a rhetorical expression rather than a sober truth when we call anything, except the resurrection, victory over death. We may conquer doubt and fear when we are dying, but that is not conquering death. It is like a warrior crushed to death by a superior antagonist refusing to yield a groan and bearing the glance of defiance to the last. You feel that he is an unconquerable spirit, but he is not the conqueror. And when you see flesh melting away, mental power becoming infantine in its feebleness, and lips scarcely able to articulate, is there left one moment a doubt upon the mind as to *who* is the conqueror in spite of all the unshaken fortitude there may be? The victory is on the side of death, not on the side of dying.

And my friends, if we would enter into the full feeling of triumph contained in this verse, we must just try to bear in mind what this world would be without the thought of a resurrection. If we could conceive an unselfish man looking upon this world of desolation with that infinite compassion that all the brave and good feel, what conception could he have but that of defeat and failure and sadness—the sons of man mounting into a bright existence, and one after another falling back into darkness and nothingness, like soldiers trying to mount an impracticable breach and falling back crushed and mangled into the ditch before the bayonets and the rattling fire of their conquerors. Misery and guilt, look which way you will, until the heart gets sick with looking at it.

Until a man looks on evil until it seems to him almost like a real personal enemy rejoicing over the destruction that it has made, he can scarcely conceive the deep rapture that rushed into the mind of the apostle Paul when he remembered that a day was coming when all this was to be reversed. A day was coming, and it was the day of reality for which he lived, ever present and ever certain, when this sad world was to put off *forever* its changefulness and its misery, and the grave was to be robbed of its victory, and the bodies were to come forth purified by their long sheep. He called all this a victory because he felt that it was a real battle that has to be fought and won before that can be secured. One battle has been fought by Christ, and another battle, most real and difficult, but yet a conquering one, is to be fought by us. He has imparted to us the virtue of His wrestlings, and the strength of His victory. So that, when the body shall rise again, the power of the law to condemn is gone because we have learned to love the law.

And now to conclude all this, there are but two things which remain to say. In the first place, if we would be conquerors, we must realize God's love in Christ. Take care not to be under the law. Constraint never yet made a conqueror. The utmost it can do it to make either a rebel or a slave. Believe that God loves you. He gave a triumphant demonstration of it in the Cross. Never shall we conquer self until we have learned *to love*. Let us remember our high privilege. Christian life, so far as it deserves the name, is victory. We are not going forth to mere battle, we are going forth to conquer. To gain mastery over self and sin and doubt and fear, until the last coldness coming across the brow tells us that all is over, and our warfare accomplished—that we are safe, the everlasting arms beneath us—*that* is our calling. Do not be content with a slothful, dreamy, uncertain struggle. You are to conquer, and the banner under which we are to win is not fear, but love. "The strength of sin is the law." The victory is by keeping before us God in Christ.

Lastly, there is need of encouragement for those of us whose faith is not of the conquering, but the timid kind. There are some whose hearts will reply to all this, Surely victory is not always a Christian's portion. Is there no cold dark watching in Christian life—no struggle when victory seems a mockery to speak of—no struggle when victory seems feeble, and Christ is to us but a name, and death a reality? "Perfect love casteth out fear" (1 John 4:18), but who has it? Victory is by faith, but, oh God, who will tell us what this faith *is* that men speak of as a thing so easy. How we are to get it! You tell us to pray for faith, but how shall we pray in earnest unless we first have the very faith we pray for?

My Christian friends, it is just to this deepest cry of the human heart that it is impossible to return a full answer. All that is true. To feel faith is the grand difficulty of life. Faith is a deep impression of God and God's love and personal trust in it. It is easy to say, "Believe on the Lord Jesus Christ, and thou shalt be saved" (Acts 16:31). But well we know it is easier said than done. We cannot say how men are to *get* faith. It is God's gift, almost in the same way that genius is. You cannot work *for* faith. You must have it first and then work *from* it.

But we can say, Look up, though we know not how the mechanism of the will which directs the eye is to be put in motion. We can say, Look to God in Christ, though we know not how men are to obtain faith to do it. Let us be in earnest. Our polar star is the love of the Cross. Take the eye off that and you are in darkness and bewilderment at once. Let us not mind what is past. Perhaps it is all failure and useless struggle and broken resolves. What then? Settle this first, friends, Are you in earnest? If so, though your faith be weak and your struggles unsatisfactory, you may begin the hymn of triumph *now,* for victory is pledged. "Thanks be to God, which" not *shall* give, but "*giveth* us the victory through our Lord Jesus Christ."

NOTES

The Inevitable Word

Clarence Edward Noble Macartney (1879–1957) ministered in Paterson, New Jersey, and Philadelphia, Pennsylvania, before assuming the influential pastorate of First Presbyterian Church, Pittsburgh, Pennsylvania, where he ministered for twenty-seven years. His preaching especially attracted men, not only to the Sunday services but also to his popular Tuesday noon luncheons. He was gifted in dealing with Bible biographies and, in this respect, has been called "the American Alexander Whyte." Much of his preaching was topical-textual, but it was always biblical, doctrinal, and practical. Perhaps his most famous sermon is "Come Before Winter."

The sermon I have selected was taken from *The Greatest Words in the Bible and in Human Speech,* published in 1938 by Cokesbury Press.

CLARENCE EDWARD NOBLE MACARTNEY

9

The Inevitable Word

It is appointed unto men once to die. (Hebrews 9:27)

WHAT IS THE INEVITABLE WORD? What is the word that to each man seems unnatural when applied to himself but natural when applied to others? What is the word that God never intended man to pronounce? What is the word that man began to speak only after he had pronounced the saddest word? What is the word that reduces all men to the same rank? What is the word that strips Dives of his millions and Lazarus of his rags? What is the word that cools avarice and stills the fires of passion? What is the word that men struggle not to pronounce, and yet all must pronounce, the prince and the peasant, the fool and the philosopher, the murderer and the saint? What is the word that none is too young to lisp and none too old or too weary to whisper? What is the word that frustrates ambition and disappoints hope, and yet a word that has the power to solve all the problems and heal all the wounds of life? What is the word that men one day shrink from, and yet on another day and in different circumstances, desire and seek after more than hid treasure? What is the word that men fear, and yet the word which, if men will listen to its voice, can teach them the meaning of all other words in life? That word is *death*. "It is appointed unto men once to die" (Heb. 9:27).

> O eloquent, just, and mighty death,
> Whom none could advise, thou hast persuaded;
> What none hath dared, thou hast done;
> And whom all the world hath flattered,
> Thou only hast cast out of the world and despised.
> Thou hast drawn together all the far stretched greatness,
> All the pride, cruelty, and ambition of man,
> And covered it all over with these two narrow words,
> *Hic Jacet.*
> —Raleigh, *History of the World*

"It is appointed unto men once to die." Toward the end of his life Daniel Webster related how once he attended divine service in a quiet country village. The clergyman was a simplehearted, pious old man. After the opening exercises he arose and pronounced his text, and then with the utmost simplicity and earnestness said, "My friends, we can die but once." "Frigid and weak as these words might seem," said Webster, "at once they were to me among the utmost impressive and awakening I ever heard." That is a striking illustration of the power of a text like this, not merely to warn men of the inevitable world and the inevitable fact, but to awaken them and to inspire them to a right kind of a life. It is with that thought in mind that in this series on *The Greatest Words in the Bible* I come tonight to "The Inevitable Word."

It is easy to think of others having to keep this appointment with death, but difficult for us to remember that we, too, must keep that appointment. "All men think all men mortal but themselves." When we see soldiers going to the front, or read of a condemned prisoner, or visit a mortally stricken man, we are conscious of a certain solemnity which gathers about such persons. But the same solemnity gathers about us, about all men. Death is appointed for all, and the question of its occurrence is merely a matter of time. Other appointments in life, the appointments of business or pleasure, we can neglect or break and take the consequence. But here is an appointment that no man can neglect, that no man can break. He can meet it only once, but he must meet it once.

> The glories of our blood and state
> Are shadows, not substantial things;
> There is no armour against fate;
> Death lays his icy hand on kings.
> Sceptre and crown
> Must tumble down,
> And in the dust be equal made
> With the poor crooked scythe and spade.
>
> —James Shirley

We have but *one* appointment with death. If it were appointed to men *twice* to die, then the first appointment would not be so important because we might hope to correct at the second appointment what was wrong in our life and in our way of meeting death at the first appointment. But death has for each of us just one rendezvous and appointment. "It is appointed unto all men once to die."

That death is the *inevitable word* certainly needs no demonstration or illustration, either in the Bible or out of it. All the facts of life proclaim it. But from the lives of men whose lives and deaths are written in the Bible, we shall show the right and the wrong way to die, how poorly or how triumphantly men keep this appointment with death.

Men Who Died in the Wrong Way

It is recorded of one of the kings of Judah, Jehoram, that when he died "he . . . departed without being desired" (2 Chron. 21:20) There was a man who kept an appointment with death in the wrong way because he had lived the wrong kind of a life. Yet he was a prince who had every advantage. He had for his father one of the best of the kings of Judah, Jehoshaphat. He had for a preacher the great prophet Elijah, who warned him when he was in the midst of his wicked reign of idolatry and murder. Yet, in spite of these advantages and these warnings, Jehoram lived the life that he had chosen to live, and when at length the end came, that is the epitaph you read upon his tomb: "He departed without being desired." No one mourned him, no one regretted that for him time was no more.

In contrast with the epitaph on the grave of this young prince is that on the grave of another, "And all Israel mourned for him" (1 Kings 14:18). This was the epitaph on the grave of Abijah. According to the popular theories of heredity and environment, Abijah ought to have been a wicked man, for he was the son of the wicked king, that king of Israel who made Israel to sin, Jeroboam, and he was brought up in that most wicked court. Yet, in spite of that heredity and environment, he lived a beautiful life. And when that life was untimely cut off as a judgment upon Jeroboam and his wife, the whole nation felt that his passing was a calamity. All Israel mourned over him. Both of these young men lived short lives. But one does not need to live long to do great good or great evil in the world. Remember, then, those two epitaphs: "He departed without being desired," and, "All Israel mourned over him." Which will you choose?

Another man who met death in the wrong way was the handsome and gifted son of David, Absalom. As a rule, the Bible tells us very little about the death and passing of either its worst or its greatest men. But there are a few exceptions, and Absalom is one of those exceptions. The story of his death and of his father's sorrow and lamentation over him is one of the most moving passages in the Bible or out of it.

What is it that we feel and think most as we listen to that cry of David over his dead and dishonored son, "O my son Absalom, my son, my son Absalom! would God I had died for thee, O Absalom, my son, my son!" (2 Sam. 18:33). What we think and feel most when we hear that cry is that a life has been wasted. We think of what the gifted and accomplished son of David might have been and what he might have done for Israel. Perhaps in David's heart, too, when he wished that he might have died in Absalom's stead, was the echo of a troubled conscience, for David must have remembered his transgressions and that prediction of the prophet Nathan at the time of David's great sin, that the sword would never depart from his house. In David's cry, too, there was that longing for death which comes to the anguished smitten soul. When Charles Sumner, the great Senator from Massachusetts, who had to drink so bitter a cup of sorrow in his own domestic life, was struck with death, there lay on his table a copy of *Henry VIII* with these lines marked by his own hand,

> Would I were dead! If God's good will were so;
> For what is in this world but care and woe!

But deeper than all else in this cry of David over Absalom is the note of lament over a wasted life. The *inevitable word* had been pronounced, the inevitable hour had come, but Absalom was not ready for it. All that he left behind him was the memory of wrong deeds and noble gifts prostituted and wasted. In the king's dale the morning sun and the moon by night gilded with splendor over the costly tomb and monument that Absalom had built for himself. But it was a tomb without a tenant, a pillar without a prince.

Another man who met the appointed hour and the appointment with death in the wrong way was that man, and the only man, whom Jesus called a fool. He is an illustration, too, of how death keeps its appointments with us when we ourselves fancy we are the furthest away from such an appointment.

This man of whom Jesus spoke in His parable had prospered greatly in the things of this world. His only worry was how to take care of his money, how to store what he had gathered. He was busy making preparations, planning to tear down his barns and build greater, and then "take it easy" in life and enjoy what he had accumulated. "Soul," he said to himself, "thou hast much goods laid up for many years; take thine ease, eat, drink, and be merry" (Luke 12:19). That was his plan, the order of his life. But his plans had a sudden interruption. God said to him, "Thou fool, this night thy soul shall be required of thee: then whose shall those things be, which thou hast provided?" (v. 20).

How powerful, how overwhelming is that saying of Jesus. Yet, alas, how many live just like that man, rejoicing in the things they have accumulated and planning for further accumulation and further enjoyment, building their hope on things. Then, suddenly, all these things are forever swept away. This night! The *inevitable word!*

Men Who Met Death's Appointment in the Right Way, or the Death of a Saint

A man who met death's appointment in the right way, and the story of whose death thrills us, inspires us, and comforts us, was the first martyr, Stephen. At first that appointment with death for Stephen seems so bitter and cruel and dark. He had lived nobly, courageously, had testified to Christ, and then is dragged out by his enemies and stoned to death. But when we hear what Stephen said, when we see what even his enemies saw in his face, when we see what Stephen saw with his dying vision, then we are encouraged, uplifted, and inspired to live as Stephen lived and to die with his faith.

The scene of Stephen's death is one of the most moving and inspiring in all the Bible. Stephen was a good man, full of the Holy Spirit, and had courageously testified to Christ and rebuked his enemies. His ability and his fidelity made him a mark for the enemies of Christ. The last words of Stephen were words of love and pity and forgiveness, for he prayed before he died, "Lord, lay not this sin to their charge" (Acts 7:60). When his enemies looked on him at his death, they saw in his face "as it had been the face of an angel" (6:15). Already death, the great destroyer and defiler, was transforming Stephen into the likeness of the heavenly glory, so that even his bruised and battered face seemed to have an angelic look about it!

But yet more striking and more moving was what Stephen himself saw as he died. He looked up steadfastly into heaven and saw the glory of God and Jesus standing on the right hand of God. In his death, forsaken and stoned by men, Stephen was not forsaken by Christ. No true believer, no faithful disciple ever is. "I will never leave thee, nor forsake thee" (Heb. 13:5). This we can count upon, that our fidelity to Christ, our obedience to His will, our testimony to His kingdom, will bring us His presence and His blessing in that inevitable appointment which we have with death.

The psalmist said, "Precious in the sight of the Lord is the death of his saints" (Ps. 116:15). The death of Stephen showed that to be true. But there is the death of another saint that shows us how precious in the sight of God such a death is and that shows us how to live and how to die. It was the death of that good woman who lived and died at Lydda, and whose name was Dorcas. She is spoken of as a "woman . . . full of good works and almsdeeds which she did" (Acts 9:36). When Peter came to the house where she had died and into the upper chamber where she lay, all the widows, all the unfortunate, stood by him in tears, each one holding up a coat or a garment that Dorcas had made for them "while she was with them" (v. 39).

How striking and full of deep meaning is that phrase "while she was with them." Her time to be with them was limited. But while she was with them she showed them her compassion and her pity and her love. She was gone. But here in these garments, sewn by her tireless hands, were the tokens of her faithful and loving life.

This is Mother's Day, and thousands of sons and daughters have recalled the name and the face and the tender and sacrificial love of their mothers. When they think of her they think of her as the friends of Dorcas remembered her, "full of good works and almsdeeds which she did" (Acts 9:36). Our mother's day with us was long with tender ministry and sacramental love. Like a blessed candle her life burned on through the darkness of the long night. Yet now in the struggles of life it seems so brief a time. But while she was with us, all that love and faith could suggest and inspire were done for us. When death at length came it did not seem a conquest, but a coronation, not an ending, but a new beginning. What could death do to such a life, but perpetuate it, enthrone it, and crown it?

I stood one day in sanctifying memories by the side of the sainted dead. Suddenly, I was conscious of the presence of another. Turning about, I saw a stranger standing near. As he seemed to be waiting for me to speak, I said to him, "Friend, who are you? And why do you intrude upon my sacred memories and reflections?" At that he answered, and with a note of impatience in his voice, "Do you not know me? I am the king of terrors."

"The king of terrors? I see nothing terrible about you."

"No, you see nothing terrible about me. For when men and women live and die as this woman lived and died, there I have no terrors at my command. My authority has vanished. But where men have lived in selfishness or impurity or strife and hatred, where they have lived for this present world and for the things of this world, and where they have lived without God and without hope, there it is that I rear my throne and dress it with such terrors as are at my command. But here I have no power and no terrors. Mortal, blessed and happy in your memories of the sainted dead. I leave you in peace."

From the realms of the blessed, and from the kingdom of the redeemed, faithful Christian mothers speak today to their sons and daughters and tell them how to live and how to die. In the midst of life's struggles and battles, they tell us to be strong. In the midst of life's temptations they tell us to be pure and true. In the midst of life's sorrows they comfort us with the recollection of their love and affection. By the inevitable gateway of death they invite us to meet with them and meet with the Lamb upon His throne in that blessed land of the leal, where they go no more out and come no more in, and where there shall be no more death. No! The *inevitable word* has given way to the Eternal Word, Life! Life! Life!

NOTES

Christ and the Fear of Death

George H. Morrison (1866–1928) assisted the great Alexander Whyte in Edinburgh, pastored two churches, and then became pastor in 1902 of the distinguished Wellington Church on University Avenue in Glasgow, Scotland. His preaching drew great crowds; in fact, people had to line up an hour before the services to be sure to get seats in the large auditorium. Morrison was a master of imagination in preaching, yet his messages are solidly biblical.

From his many published volumes of sermons, I have chosen this message, found in *The After-Glow of God,* published in 1912 by Hodder and Stoughton, London.

GEORGE H. MORRISON

10

Christ and the Fear of Death

And deliver them, who through fear of death were all their lifetime subject to bondage. (Hebrews 2:15)

THERE ARE TWO FEELINGS that the thought of death has ever kindled in the human breast, and the first of them is curiosity. Always in the presence of that veil, through which sooner or later we all pass, men have been moved to ask, with bated breath, What is it which that veil conceals? It is as if the most diaphanous of curtains were hung between our eyes and the great secret, making men the more wistful to interpret it. It has been said by a well-known Scottish essayist that this would account for the crowd at executions. You know how the people used to flock in thousands when a criminal was to die upon the gallows. And Alexander Smith throws out this thought that it was not just savagery which brought them there. It was the unappeasable curiosity which death forever stirs in human hearts.

But if the thought of death moves our curiosity, there is another feeling that is ever linked with it. Death is not alone the source of wonder. Death has ever been the source of fear. How universal that feeling is we see from this, that we share it with all animate creation. Wherever there is life in any form there is an instinct that recoils from death. When the butterfly evades the chasing schoolboy—when the stag turns at bay against the dogs—we have the rudiments of that which in a loftier sphere may grow to be a bondage and a tyranny. The fear of death is not a religious thing, although religion has infinitely deepened it. It is as old as existence, as wide as the whole world, and as lofty and deep as the whole social fabric. It touches the savage in the heart of Africa, as every reader of Dr. Livingstone knows, and it hides under the mantle of the prince as well as under the jacket of the prodigal. How keenly it was felt in the old world, every reader of pagan literature has seen. The aim and object of the old philosophy was largely to crush it out of human life. In the great and gloomy poem of Lucretius, in many a page of Cicero, above all in the treatises of Plutarch and of Seneca, we learn what a mighty thing the fear of death was with the men and women of the Roman Empire.

Of course I do not mean that the fear of death is always active and present and insistent. To say that would be exaggeration and would be untrue to the plain facts of life. When a man is in the enjoyment of good health, he very rarely thinks of death at all. When the world goes well with him and he is happy, he has the trick of forgetting he is mortal. He digs his graves within the garden walls and covers them with a wealth of summer flowers so that the eye scarce notices the mound when the birds are singing in the trees. We know, too, how a passion or enthusiasm will master the fear of death within the heart. A soldier in the last rush will never think of it, though comrades are dropping on every side of him. And a timid mother, for her little child's sake, or a woman for the sake of one she loves, will face the deadliest peril without trembling. For multitudes the fear of death is dormant or else life would be unbearable and wretched. But though it is dormant, it is always there, ready to be revived in the last day. In times of shipwreck—in hours of sudden panic—when we are ill and told we may not live, then shudderingly, as from uncharted deeps, there steals on men this universal terror. Remember there is nothing cowardly in that. A man may be afraid and be a hero. There are times when to feel no terror is not courage. It is but the hallmark of insensibility. It is not what a man feels that makes the difference. It is how he handles and orders what he feels. It is the spirit in which he holds himself in the hour when the heart is overwhelmed.

Nor can we be altogether blind to the purposes which God meant this fear to serve. Like everything universal in the heart, it has its office in the plans of heaven. You remember the cry wrung from the heart of Keats in his so exquisite music to the nightingale. "Full many a time," he sings, "I have been half in love with easeful death." And it may be that there are some here tonight who have been at times so weary of it all that they too have been in love with easeful death. It may have been utter tiredness that caused it. It may have been something deeper than all weariness. Who knows but that even here before me there be not someone who has dreamed of suicide? It is from all such thoughts, and from all the passion to have done with life, that we are rescued and redeemed and guarded by the terror that God has hung around the grave. Work may be hard, but death is harder still. Duty may be stern, but death is sterner. Dark and gloomy may be the unknown tomorrow, but it is not so dark and gloomy as the grave. Who might not break the hedge and make for liberty were the hedge easy to be pushed aside? But God has hedged us about with many a thorn—and we turn to our little pasturage again.

When Adam and Eve had been expelled from Eden, they must have longed intensely to return. It was so beautiful and the world so desolate; it was so fertile and the world so hard. But ever, when they clasped repentant hands and stole in the twilight to the gate of Paradise, there rose the awful form with flaming sword. Sleepless and vigilant he stood at watch. His was a dreadful and terrific presence. No human heart could face that living fire which stood in guardianship of what was lost. And that was why God had placed His angel there, that they might be driven back to the harsh furrow and till the soil and rise into nobility while the sweat was dropping from the brow. So are we driven back to life again by the terror which stands sentinel on death. So are we driven to our daily cross, however unsupportable it seems. And bearing it, at first because we must, it comes to blossom with the passing days, until we discover that on this side the grave there is more of paradise than we had dreamed. Christ, then, does *not* deliver us from the deep instinct of self-preservation. That is implanted in the heart by God. It is given for the safeguarding of His gift. It is only when that fear becomes a bondage, and when that instinct grows into a tyranny, that Christ steps in and breaks the chains that bind us and sets our trembling feet in a large room. The question is, then, how did He do that? How has Christ liberated us from this bondage? I shall answer that by trying to distinguish three elements that are inherent in that fear.

In the first place, our fear is in a measure but a fear of dying. It is not the fact of death that terrifies, it is all that we associate with the fact. We may have seen some deathbed that was a scene of agony. It is a memory that we shall never lose. We may have read, in novel or in drama, a story of torment in the closing hours. And it is not what death leads to or removes, but rather that dark accompanying prospect that lies hidden within a thousand hearts as an element of the terror of the grave. I think I need hardly stop to prove to you that this is an unreasonable fear. If there are deathbeds that are terrible, are there not others that are quiet as sleep? But blessed be God, Christ does not only comfort us when we are terrified with *just* alarms, He comforts us when we are foolish children. Girt with mortality, He says to us, "Take therefore no thought for the morrow" (Matt. 6:34). Dreading the pain that one day may arrive, He says, "Sufficient unto the day is the evil thereof" (v. 34). He never prayed, "Give us a sight of death and help us to contemplate it every hour we live." He prayed, "Give us this day our daily bread" (Matt. 6:11). Christ will not have us stop the song today because of the possible suffering tomorrow. If we have grace to live by when we need it, we shall have grace to die by when we need it. And so He sets His face against that element and says to us, "Let not your heart be troubled" (John 14:1, 27). "My grace is sufficient for thee: for my strength is made perfect in weakness" (2 Cor. 12:9).

Secondly, much of our fear of death springs from the thought that death is the end of everything. It is always pitiful to say farewell, and there is no farewell like that of death. You remember how Charles Lamb uttered that feeling with the wistful tenderness that makes us love him. He did not want to leave this kindly world, nor his dear haunts, nor the familiar faces. And deep within us, though we may not acknowledge it, there is that factor in the fear of death—the passionate clinging of the human heart to the only life that it has known. We have grown familiar with it in the years. It has come to look on us with friendly eyes. It has been a glad thing to have our work to do, and human love and friendship have been sweet. And then comes death and takes all that away from us and says it never shall be ours again. We brood on it and are lonely and afraid. Thanks be to God, *that* factor in the fear has been destroyed by Jesus Christ. For He has died and is risen again, and He is the first-fruits of them that sleep. And if the grave for Him was not an end, but only an incident in life eternal, then we may rest assured that in His love there is no such sadness as the broken melody. All we have striven to be we shall attain. All we have striven to do we shall achieve. All we have loved shall meet us once again with eyes that are transfigured in the dawn. Every purpose that was baffled here and every love that never was fulfilled, all that, and all our labor glorified, shall still be ours when shadows flee away. This life is but the prelude to the piece. This life is the introduction to the book. It is not *finis* we should write at death. It is not *finis,* it is *initium.* And that is how Jesus Christ has met this element and mastered it in His victorious way and made it possible for breaking hearts to bear the voiceless sorrow of farewell.

Thirdly, much of the fear of death springs from the certainty of coming judgment. Say what you will, you know as well as I do that there is a day of judgment still to come. Conscience tells it, if conscience be not dead. The very thought of a just God demands it. Unless there be a judgment still to come, life is the most tragical of mockeries. And every voice of antiquity proclaims it, and every savage tribe within the forest and with a certainty that never wavered it was proclaimed by the Lord Jesus Christ. Well may you and I fear death, if "it is appointed unto men once to die, but after this the judgment" (Heb. 9:27). Seen to our depths, with every secret known, we are all to stand before Almighty God. Kings will be there, and peasants will be there, and you and I who are not kings nor peasants. And the rich and the poor will meet together there, for the Lord is the maker of them all. It is that thought which makes death so terrible. It is that which deepens the horror of the tomb. Dwell on that coming day beyond the grave, and what a prospect of affright it is! And it is then that Jesus Christ appears and drives these terrors to the winds of heaven. He says to the vilest sinner here tonight, "Son of man, stand upon thy feet" (Ezek. 2:1). "He that believeth on me *hath* everlasting life" (John 6:47). He gives us our acquittal here and now. He tells us that for every man who trusts Him "there is therefore now no condemnation" (Rom. 8:1). And He tells us that because He died for us, and because He bore our sins up to the tree, and because He loves us with a love so mighty that neither life nor death can tear us from it. That is the faith to live by and to die by: "I will both lay me down in peace, and sleep" (Ps. 4:8). That is the faith which makes us more than conquerors over the ugliest record of our past. "O death, where is thy sting? O grave, where is thy victory? . . . Thanks be to God, which giveth us the victory through our Lord Jesus Christ" (1 Cor. 15:55, 57).

NOTES

The Shortness of Life

Phillips Brooks (1835–1893) was ordained into the Protestant Episcopal Church in 1860 while serving in Philadelphia. He became minister of Trinity Church, Boston, in 1869, and served there for twenty-two years. In 1891 he was ordained Bishop of Massachusetts. He is best known for his *Lectures on Preaching,* which he delivered at Yale in 1877. He published many volumes of sermons and lectures.

This sermon was taken from *Sermons* by Phillips Brooks, published in 1879 by Richard D. Dickinson, London.

11

The Shortness of Life

Brethren, the time is short. (1 Corinthians 7:29)

THE TONE IN WHICH a man speaks often helps us to understand his meaning quite as much as the actual words he says. And with a great and sincere writer there is a tone in writing as well as in speaking, something which gives an intonation to the words he writes and lets us understand in which of several possible spirits he has written them. "Brethren, the time is short," writes St. Paul to the Corinthians, and there is no tremor of dismay or sadness in his voice. He was in the midst of work, full of the interest and joy of living, holding the reins of many complicated labors in his hands, and he quietly said, "This is not going to last long. Very soon it will be over." It is what men often say to themselves with terror, clutching the things which they hold all the more closely, as if they would hold on to them forever. There is nothing of that about St. Paul. And on the other hand, there is nothing of morbidness or discontent, no rejoicing that the time is short and wishing that it was still shorter. There is no hatred of life that makes him want to be away. There is no mad impatience for the things that lie beyond. There is simply a calm and satisfied recognition of a fact. There is a reasonable sense of what is good and dear in life and, yet, at the same time, of what must lie beyond life, of what life cannot give us.

It is as when the same pen wrote those sublime and simple

words, "This corruptible must put on incorruption, and this mortal must put on immortality" (1 Cor. 15:53). The quiet statement of a great, eternal necessity at which the wise man must feel the same kind of serious joy as that with which he follows the movements of the stars, and looks to see day and night inevitably give place to one another. Or it is like that calm, majestic weighing of two worlds over against each other and letting his will lie in even balance between them, cordially waiting the will of God with which the same Paul wrote again, "I am in a strait betwixt two, having a desire to depart, and to be with Christ; which is far better: nevertheless to abide in the flesh is more needful for you. And having this confidence, I know that I shall abide" (Phil. 1:23–25). Or, again, it is like the healthy satisfaction of the healthy boy in his boyhood, knowing all the time the manhood that awaits him, feeling his boyhood pressed upon by it, hoping for it and expecting it, but living now in the concentrated happiness and work of the years whose activity and pleasure is all the more intense because of the sense that it must end.

It does not matter what St. Paul was thinking of when he said the time was short. He may have had his mind upon the death that they were all approaching. He may have thought of the coming of Christ, which he seems to have expected to take place while he was yet alive. I do not think we can be certain which it was. And perhaps the very vagueness about this helps us to his meaning. For he is not, evidently, dwelling upon the nature of the event that is to limit the "time," only upon the simple fact that there is a limit. He is dwelling upon the fact that the period of earthly life and work lies like an island in the midst of a greater sea of being—the island of time in the ocean of a timeless eternity—and that it is pressed upon and crowded into littleness by the infinite. Not the shore where the sea sets the island its limits, but only the island in the sea, hearing the sea always on its shores. Not the experience by which this life should pass into another, but only the compression and intensifying of this life by the certainty that there is another. Not death, but the shortness of life—that is what his thoughts are fixed upon, and it is this of which the best men always think the most.

Our theme is this, then—the shortness of human life. How old that theme is, how trite, and oftentimes how dreary. As we look back and listen we hear all the generations wearisomely wasting their little span of life in doleful lamentations that it is not longer. Trite lessons that nobody loves to learn, dull poems that no man can sing, efforts at resignation that do not succeed—these are what come flocking up about the truth that life is short. It is the ghost at the banquet of human thought. It is the monotonous, miserable undertone that haunts all the bustle and clatter of men's work and all the gay music of their pleasure making. I wish that I could read its truth to you in another tone and paint its picture in another color. I wish that I could make you hear it as it seems as if Paul's Corinthians must have heard it, almost like a trumpet—a call to work and joy. If we can catch his spirit at all, something of that may certainly be possible.

And first, then, let us ask, What is the shortness of life? What do we mean by life's being short? There is a little insect that crawls upon the trees and creeps in one short day of ours through all the experiences of life from birth to death. In a short twenty-four hours his life begins, matures, and ends—birth, youth, activity, age, decrepitude, all crowded and compressed into these moments that slip away uncounted in one day of our human life. Is his life long or short? Is our life long or short to him? If he could realize it by any struggle of his insect brain, what an eternity our threescore years and ten must seem to him! And then lift up your eyes, lift up your thoughts, and think of God. What look has any life that has any limits to Him? Nothing short of eternity can seem long to Him. He sees the infant's life flash like a ripple into the sunlight of existence and vanish almost before the eye has caught it. And He sees Methuselah's slow existence creep through its nine hundred and sixty-nine years and find, at last, the grave that had stood waiting so long. Is there a real difference in the length of these two lives to Him? A little longer ripple is the life of the patriarch than was the life of the baby, that is all.

What do we mean, then, by the shortness of our human life? To the ephemera it looks like an eternity; to God it looks like an instant. Evidently these attributes of length and shortness must be relative; they are not absolute. How shall human life seem, then, to man? Must it not depend altogether upon where he stands to look at it? If he stands with the ephemera, his life looks long to him. If he stands with God, his life looks short to him. If a man is able, that is, to conceive of immortality; if he can picture to himself a being who can live forever; if he recognizes in himself any powers which can outlast and laugh at death—then any limit of life must seem narrow. Against the broad background of the whole, any part must seem small. On the blue sky the almost million miles of the sun's breadth seem narrow. It is here that the truth about the matter lies. It is only by the dim sense of his immortality, only by the divine sight of himself as a being capable of long, long life, that man thinks his life on earth is short. Only by losing that divine sight of himself and looking at himself as the beasts look at themselves can he come to think his life long. The beast's life never seems short to him. Think of yourself as a beast and your life will never seem short to you. It is the divine consciousness in man, the consciousness that he is a child of God, that makes him know he is short-lived. Human life is not long or short absolutely. It seems short to us because the consciousness of immortality is in us. What then? It could not seem long unless we threw that consciousness away. That we can count it short, then, is the pledge and witness of our nobility. The man who died among us yesterday, oh, realize, my friends, that the very fact that his life could seem to you, as you stood by his coffin, to have been very short, is a sign that you have been able to conceive of his humanity and yours being immortal. Feel this, and is not the shortness of life the crown and glory of our race?

And again, we all know how the shortness of life is bound up with its fullness. It is to him who is most active, always thinking, feeling, working, caring for people and for things, that life seems short. Strip a life empty and it will seem long enough. The day crawls to the idler and flies to the busy worker. That is the commonplace of living. The shortness of life is closely associated, not merely with the great hopes of the future, but with the real vitality of the present. What then? If you and I complain how short life is, how quick it flies through the grasp with which we try to hold it, we are complaining of that which is the necessary consequence of our vitality. You can make life long only by making it slow. If you want to make it slow, I should think that there were men enough in town who could tell you how. Men with idle hands and brains who seem to have so much trouble to get through life as it is that we cannot imagine that they really wish that there were more of it.

And tell me, then, does not the shortness of life cease to be our sorrow and lamentation? Does it not become our crown and privilege and glory when we see that life is short to us because we are—that life is short to us just in proportion as we are—conscious of immortality and full of vitality? Who would not dread to have his life begin to seem long? Who would not feel that he was losing the proof-marks of his best humanity, forgetting that he was immortal and ceasing to be thoroughly alive?

But let us leave this and go further on. Suppose a man, with more or less of a struggle and with what grace he can, has accepted the shortness of life as a conviction. He knows it. It has been forced upon him by some special shock, or it has been pressed into him by his gradual experience, the certainty that life is short, that he is not to be, cannot be, a long time here on the earth. What effect will that conviction have upon his life? What effect ought it to have? Evidently it ought to go deeper than his spirits. It ought to do something more than make him glad or sorry. It ought to have some effect upon his conduct and his character. I should like to suggest to you in several particulars what it seems to me that that effect will be.

First of all, must it not make a man try to sift the things that offer themselves to him and try to find out what his things are? The indiscriminateness of most men's lives impresses us, I think, more and more. The old Greek Epictetus said that for each of men there is one great classification of the universe into the things that concern him and the things that do not concern him. To how many men that classification is all vague. Many men's souls are like omnibuses, stopping to take up every interest or task that holds up its finger and beckons them from the sidewalk. So many men are satisfied with asking themselves vague questions about whether this thing or that thing is wrong, as if whatever they could not pronounce to be absolutely wrong for every man to do was right for them to do. So many men seem to think it enough that they should see no good reason for not doing a thing in order to justify their doing it. As if the absence of any reason why they should do it were not reason enough why they should not do it. Such indiscriminateness would be inevitable, you could not hope to control it, if life were indefinitely long.

Such indiscriminateness is almost legitimate and necessary in childhood, in the beginning, the freshman year of life. Then life seems endless. Then the quick experimenting senses are ready for whatever strikes them. But as the course goes on, as its limit comes in sight and we see how short it is, the elective system must come in. Out of the mass of things that we have touched, we must choose those that are ours—the books that we shall read, the men whom we shall know, the power that we shall wield, the pleasure that we shall enjoy, the special point where we shall drop our bit of usefulness into the world's life before we go. We come to be like a party of travelers left at a great city railway station for a couple of hours. All cannot see everything in town. Each has to choose according to his tastes what he will see. They separate into their individualities instead of going wandering about promiscuously, as they would if there were no limit to their time. So conscientiousness, self-knowledge, independence, and the toleration of other men's freedom which always goes with the most serious and deep assertion of our own freedom are closely connected with the sense that life is very short.

But again, besides this discrimination of the things with which we ought to deal, the sense of the shortness of life also brings a power of freedom in dealing with the things which we do take to be our own. This, I think, is what St. Paul is speaking of in the words which are in close connection with this text of ours. "Brethren, the time is short," he says. "It remaineth, that both they that have wives be as though they had none; and they that weep, as though they wept not; and they that rejoice, as though they rejoiced not; and they that buy, as though they possessed not; and they that use this world, as not abusing it: for the fashion of this world passeth away" (1 Cor. 7:29–31). Not that they should not marry or weep or rejoice or buy or use the world. The shortness of life was not to paralyze life like that. But they were to do these things as if they did them not. They were to do them with a soul above their details, and in the principles, reasons, and motives that lay beyond them.

To take once more the illustration of the travelers: he who has only an hour to stay in some great foreign city will not puzzle and burden himself with all the intricacies of its streets or all the small particulars of its life. He will try, if he is wise, simply to catch its general spirit, to see what sort of town it is, and learn its lessons. He must tread its pavements, ride in its carriages, talk with its people, but he will not do these things as the citizens do them. He will not be fastidious about them. He will hold them very loosely, only trying to make each of them give him what help it can toward the understanding of the city. He will do them as if he did them not. Is not that the idea? Just so he who knows he is in the world for a very little while, who knows it and feels it, is not like a man who is to live here forever. He strikes for the center of living. He cares for the principles and not for the forms of life. He does the little daily things of life, but he does them for their purposes, not for themselves. He is like a climber on a rocky pathway who sets his foot upon each projecting point of stone, but who treads on each, not for its own sake, but for the sake of the ones above it.

The man who knows he is to die tomorrow does all the acts of today, but does them as if he did not do them, does them freely, cannot be a slave to their details, has entered already into something of the large liberty of death. That is the way in which the sense that life is short liberates a man from the slavery of details. You say, perhaps, "That is not good. No man can do his work well unless his heart is in it." But is it not also true that a man's heart can really be only in the heart of his work and that the most conscientious faithfulness in details will always belong to the man, not who serves the details, but who serves the idea of the work which he has to do? He who holds that the "fashion of this world passeth away" (v. 31) will live in the fashion still as a present means of working, but will get a great deal more out of it because he holds it a great deal more loosely than the man who treats it as if it were to last forever. Through the freer use of the fashion that passes away he will come to the substance that cannot pass away—the love of God, the life and character of man.

Closely connected with this is another idea, which is that in the shortness of life the great emotions and experiences by which the human character is ruled and shaped assume their largest power and act with their most ennobling influence. Every emotion that a man can feel, every experience that a man can undergo has its little form and its great form. Happiness is either a satisfaction that the cushions are soft and the skies clear, or a sublime content in harmony with the good universe of God. Love is either a whim of the eyes or a devotion and consecration of the soul. Self-confidence is either a petty pride in our own narrowness or a realization of our duty and privilege as one of God's children. Hope is either a petty willfulness or a deep and thoughtful insight. Trust is either laziness or love. Fear is either a fright of the nerves or the solemn sense of the continuousness and necessary responsibility of life. And grief is either the wrench of a broken habit or the agony of a wrung soul. So every emotion has its higher and its lower forms. It means but little to me if I know only that a man is happy or unhappy, if I do not know of what sort his joy or sorrow is. But all the emotions are certainly tempted to larger action if it is realized that the world in which they take their birth is but for a little time, that its fashion passes away, that the circumstances of an experience are very transitory. That must drive me down into the very essence of every experience and make me realize it in the profoundest and largest way.

Take, for instance, one experience. Think of deep sorrow coming to a man, something which breaks his home and heart by taking suddenly, or slowly, out of them that which is the center of them both, some life around which all his life has lived. There are two forms in which the sorrow of that death comes to a man. One is in the change of circumstances, the breaking up of sweet companionships and pleasant habits, the loneliness and weariness of living. The other is in the solemn brooding of mystery over the soul and the tumult of love within the soul, the mystery of death, the distress of love. Now if the man who is bereaved sees nothing in the distance as he looks forward but one stretch of living, if he realizes most how long life is, it is the first of these aspects of his sorrow that is the most real to him. He multiplies the circumstances of his bereavement into all these coming years. Year after year, year after year, he is to live alone. But if, as it so often happens when death comes very near to us, life seems a very little thing if, when we stand to watch the spirit which has gone away from earth to heaven, the years of earth which we have yet to live seem very few and short. If it seems but a very little time before we shall go too, then our grief is exalted to its largest form. It grows unselfish. It is perfectly consistent with a triumphant thankfulness for the dear soul that has entered into rest and glory. It dwells not on the circumstances of bereavement but upon that mysterious strain in which love has been stretched from this world to the other, and, amid all the pain that the tension brings, is still aware of joy at the new knowledge of its own capacities which has been given it.

Ah, you must all know, you must all have seen, that men's griefs are as different as men's lives are. To the man who is all wrapped up in this world, grief comes as the ghosts come to the poor narrow-minded churl—to plague and tease him, to disturb the circumstances and habits of his living, to pull down his fences, and make strange, frightful noises in his quiet rooms. All is petty. To him to whom life is but an episode, a short stage in the existence of eternity, who is always cognizant of the great surrounding world of mystery, grief comes as angels came to the tent of Abraham. Laughter is hushed before them. The mere frolic of life stands still, but the soul takes the grief in as a guest, meets it at the door, kisses its hand, washes its travel-stained feet, spreads its table with the best food, gives it the seat by the fireside, and listens reverently for what it has to say about the God from whom it came. So different are the sorrows that come to two men which seem just the same. So is every emotion great or little, according to the life in which it finds its play. It must find earth too small for it and open eternity to itself, or it spreads itself out thin and grows petty. I beg you, if God sends you grief, to take it largely by letting it first of all show you how short life is and then prophesy eternity. Such is the grief of which the poet sings so nobly:

> Grief should be
> Like joy, majestic, equable, sedate;
> Confirming, cleansing, raising, making free;
> Strong to consume all troubles; to commend
> Great thoughts, grave thoughts, thoughts lasting to the end.

But grief, to be all that, must see the end. Grief must bring and forever keep with its pain such a sense of the shortness of life that the pain shall seem but a temporary accident, and that all that is to stay forever after the pain has ceased—the exaltation, the unselfishness, the mystery, the nearness to God—shall seem to be the substance of the sorrow.

But let me hasten on and name another power that seems to be bound up with the perception of the shortness of life. I mean the criticalness of life. All men who have believed at all that there was another life have held in some way that this life was critical. Some have held absolutely that probation wholly stopped when this life ended, and that as the man was when he died, so he was certainly to be forever and ever. Others have only felt that such a change as death involves must have some mighty power to fasten character, and so to fasten destiny, and that the soul, living in any unknown world, must carry forever, deep in its nature and its fortunes, the marks and consequences of what it has been here. That thought of criticalness belongs to every limited period of being which opens into something greater. A boy feels the probation character of his youth, feels that he is making manhood, just in proportion as he vividly realizes the approach of his majority. And man is made so that some sense of criticalness is necessary to the most vigorous and best life always. Let me feel that nothing but this moment depends upon this moment's action, and I am very apt to let this moment act pretty much as it will. Let me see the spirits of the moments yet unborn standing and watching it anxiously, and I must watch it also for their sakes. And it is in this general sense of probation, or of criticalness, this sense that no moment lives or dies to itself—it is in this, not stated as doctrine, but spread out as a great pervading consciousness all through life—it is in this that the strongest moral power of life is found.

Now ask yourself: Could this have been if life had been so

long, if life had seemed so long to men, as never to suggest its limits? It is when the brook begins to hear the great river calling it, and knows that its time is short, that it begins to hurry over the rocks and toss its foam into the air and make straight for the valley. Life that never thinks of its end lives in a present and loses the flow and movement of responsibility. It is not so much that the shortness of life makes us prepare for death as it is that it spreads the feeling of criticalness all through life and makes each moment prepare for the next, makes life prepare for life. This is its power. Blessed is he who feels it. Blessed is he in whose experience each day and each hour has all the happiness and all the solemnity of a parent toward the day and the hour to which it gives birth, stands sponsor for it, holds it for baptism at the font of God. Such days are sacred in each other's eyes. The life in which such days succeed each other is a holy family, with its moments "bound each to each by natural piety."

I take one moment only to suggest one more consequence which comes from the sense of how short life is. I mean the feeling that it gives us toward our fellowmen. Do you not know that when your time of relationship is short with any man, your relations with that man grow true and deep? Two men who have lived side by side for years, with business and social life between them, with a multitude of suspicions and concealments, let them know that they have only an hour more to live together, and, as they look into each other's eyes, do not the suspicions and concealments clear away? They know each other. They trust each other. They think the best of each other. They are ready to do all that they can do for each other in those few moments that remain. Oh, my dear friends, you who are letting miserable misunderstandings run on from year to year, meaning to clear them up some day. You who are keeping wretched quarrels alive because you cannot quite make up your mind that now is the day to sacrifice your pride and kill them. You who are passing men sullenly upon the street, not speaking to them out of some silly spite, and yet knowing that it would fill you with shame and remorse if you heard that one of those men were dead tomorrow morning. You who are letting your neighbor starve until you hear that he is dying of starvation, or letting your friend's heart ache for a word of appreciation or sympathy, which you mean to give him some day—if you could only know and see and feel, all of a sudden, that "the time is short," how it would break the spell. How you would go instantly and do the thing which you might never have another chance to do. What a day of friendliness, of brotherliness, of reconciliations, of help the last day of the world will be if men shall know how near the awful end is! But need we wait for that? Cannot the men and women whom we live with now be sacred to us by the knowledge of what wonderful, mysterious ground it is that we are walking together, here in this narrow human life, close on the borders of eternity?

"Brethren, the time is short." There is the fact, then, forever pressing on us, and these are the consequences which it ought to bring to those who feel its pressure. Behold, it is no dreary shadow hanging about our heads and shutting out the sunshine. It is an everlasting inspiration. It makes a man know himself and his career. It makes him put his heart into the heart of the career that he knows to be his. It makes the emotions and experiences of life great and not petty to him. It makes life solemn and interesting with criticalness. It makes friendship magnanimous, and the desire to help our fellowmen real and energetic. It concentrates and invigorates our lives. In the brightest, freshest, clearest mornings, it comes to us not as a cloud, not as a paralysis, but as a new brightness in the sunshine and a new vigor in the arm. "Brethren, the time is short." Only remember the shortness of life is not a reality to us, except as it shows itself against a true realization of eternity. Life is long to any man, however life mourns over its shortness, to whom life is a whole. Life as a part, life set upon the background of eternity, life recognized as the temporary form of that whose substance is everlasting, that is short. We wait for, we expect its end. And remember that to the Christian the interpretation of all this is in the Incarnation of Jesus Christ. "I am he that liveth, and was dead; and, behold, I am alive for evermore" (Rev. 1:18). The earthly life set against the eternal life, the incorporate earthly form uttering here for a time the everlasting and essential being, those years shut in out of the eternities between the birth and the ascension, that resurrection opening the prospect of the life that never was to end—these are the never-failing interpretation to the man who believes in them of the temporal and eternal in his own experience.

Christ comes and puts His essential life into our human form. In that form He claims the truest brotherhood with us. He shares our lot. He binds His life with ours so that they never can be separated. What He is we must be; what we are He must be forever. Finally, by the cross of love, He, entering into our death, takes us completely into His life. And when He had done all this He rose. Out of His tomb, standing there among human tombs, He comes, and lo! before Him there rolls on the unbroken endlessness of being. And not before Him alone—before those also whom He had taken so completely to Himself. His resurrection makes our resurrection sure. Our earthly life, like His, becomes an episode, a short, special, temporary thing, when it is seen like His against an immortality.

So the Incarnation is the perpetual interpretation of our life. Jesus cries, "It is finished" (John 19:30), on His cross, and at once it is evident that that finishing is but a beginning—that it is a breaking to pieces of the temporal, that it may be lost in the eternal! That cross is the perpetual glorification of the shortness of life. In its light we, too, can stand by the departing form of our own life or of some brother's life, and say, "It is finished," and know that the finishing is really a beginning. The temporary is melting away like a cloud in the sky, that the great total sky may all be seen. The form in which the man has lived is decaying, that the real life of the man may be apparent. The fashion of this world is passing away. The episode, the accident of earth, is over that the spiritual reality may be clear. It is in the light of the Cross that the exquisite picture of Shelley, who tried so hard to be heathen and would still be Christian in his own despite, is really realized:

> The one remains, the many change and pass;
> Heaven's light forever shines; earth's shadows fly;
> Life, like a dome of many-colour'd glass,
> Stains the white radiance of eternity,
> Until death tramples it to fragments.

And so what is there to be done? What could be clearer? Only to him who realizes eternity does the short human life really seem short and give out of its shortness its true solemnity and blessing. It is only by binding myself to eternity that I can know the shortness of time. But how shall I bind myself to eternity except by giving myself to Him who is eternal in obedient love? Obedient love! Loving obedience! That is what binds the soul of the less to the soul of the greater everywhere. I give myself to the eternal Christ and in His eternity I find my own. In His service I am bound to Him and the shortness of that life, whose limitations in any way shut me out from Him, becomes an inspiration not a burden to me. Oh, my dear friends, you who with Christian faith have seen a Christian die, tell me was not this short life then revealed to you in all its beauty? Did you not see completely that no life was too long which Christ had filled with the gift and knowledge of himself. No life was too short which departed from the earth only to go and be with Him in heaven forever?

My dear friends, let us think how solemn, how beautiful, the thought of dedication to Christ becomes, when through His voice which calls us sounds the warning and inspiring cry of His disciple, "Brethren, the time is short." There is no time to waste of what belongs entirely to Him. "The time is short." Take your place now. Bind yourself now with the fortunes of those who are trying to serve Him. This Christian church which we see here is only the beginning. This poor, stained, feeble church of earth is only the germ and promise of the great church of heaven. We who are trying to serve Him together now have a right to take courage from the promise of the Master, who has overcome. "Him that overcometh will I make a pillar in the temple of my God, and he shall go no more out" (Rev. 3:12).

NOTES

The Vanquished Enemy

George Campbell Morgan (1863–1945) was the son of a British Baptist preacher and preached his first sermon when he was thirteen years old. He had no formal training for the ministry, but his tireless devotion to the study of the Bible helped him to become one of the leading Bible teachers of his day. Rejected by the Methodists, he was ordained into the Congregational ministry. He was associated with Dwight L. Moody in the Northfield Bible conferences and as an itinerant Bible teacher. He is best known as the pastor of the Westminster Chapel, London (1904–1917 and 1933–1945). During his second term at Westminster Chapel, Dr. D. Martyn Lloyd-Jones was his associate.

Morgan published more than sixty books and booklets, and his sermons are found in *The Westminster Pulpit* (London: Hodder and Stoughton, 1906–1916). This sermon was taken from *26 Sermons by Dr. G. Campbell Morgan,* volume 2, published by College Press, Joplin, Missouri, in the Evangelical Reprint Library series.

GEORGE CAMPBELL MORGAN

12

The Vanquished Enemy

The last enemy that shall be abolished is death.
(1 Corinthians 15:26 ASV)

TONIGHT I CAST MYSELF upon the patience and sympathy of my congregation. I speak out of an almost choking sense of sorrow and bereavement. "The air seems full of farewells to the dying."

The week before last, my old personal friend and comrade in the ministry, the man who was ordained in the same year as I was, was with me in London joyfully participating in our denominational meetings and celebrations. He left me on Saturday and was met on reaching home by his boy whom I had known since babyhood. He had just reached twenty-one years of age and was full of life and promise, a rare and beautiful realization of sane and sanctified young manhood. On Sunday morning last he sickened, and by four o'clock on Monday morning God had kissed him into the light. On Wednesday I traveled down, stood by my friend, and committed the sacred body of his boy to the dust. Tonight my friend is with me, a bereaved and sorrowing man.

Next Sunday night, Thomas Nicholson, who commenced his ministry at Paddington in the same year that I commenced mine at Westminster, was to have stood at this desk and preached to my congregation. A week ago on Thursday he retired to rest, and on the following Monday morning passed away from the earthly service.

How can a man escape from the oppression of these things. They are common enough, I know. I suppose no Sunday passes without there being some in this house who are face to face with the grim and ghastly fact of death. Perhaps, therefore, it is good that I should be compelled ever and anon to face it also. Therefore, tonight, while speaking largely to my own heart, I hope and pray that I may minister strength and comfort to others also.

To know Christ with any measure of intimacy is to be compelled to think of everything in His presence. There is no better way of facing the fact of death in His company than in the atmosphere of this great chapter which I read in your hearing, constituting, as it does, an anthem of heaven and the dirges of earth.

At the very heart of the chapter I find my text. It is almost an exclamatory parenthesis. If you should read this chapter anew and should leave out my text, there would be no break in the argument. Indeed the break in the argument is created by the presence of the text. "For he must reign, till he hath put all his enemies under his feet. . . . For, He put all things in subjection under his feet" (1 Cor. 15:25-27). So the words run with my text omitted, and the statement is coherent, and perfect in itself. In the midst of it, the apostle broke out into these words, "The last enemy that shall be abolished is death."

The words ring true to human sensibility. Death is not robed in garments of beauty. It is named an enemy. Its long persistent power is recognized. It is the *last* enemy to be abolished. Nevertheless the exclamation occurs in the midst of great words, vibrant with victory. "He must reign, till he hath put all his enemies under his feet."

Then let us think of death in this setting; of death as an enemy; of the abolition of death. Then let us reverently attempt to deduce from the twofold line of consideration what the Christian spirit should be in the presence of death.

First, then, death as an enemy. Paul's word is suggestive and leaves no room for doubt as to his meaning. Our translators have accurately rendered it *enemy* for lack of any word that will more accurately express the thought of the word itself. The word that Paul employed means quite literally that which is hateful and that which is hostile—that which is hateful because it is hostile, a veritable enemy.

The common human attitude toward death is exactly expressed in that apostolic description of it. In another of the New Testament writers the author refers to men saying of them, "Them who through fear of death were all their lifetime subject to bondage" (Heb. 2:15). How true is that description! We of the Christian faith challenge death, and rightly so, as I hope to show: "O death, where is thy victory? O death, where is thy sting?" (1 Cor. 15:55). That is the cry of faith following and resulting from the declaration: "Death is swallowed up in victory!" (v. 54). But that is not yet. If we place the declaration in its true setting we discover that the apostle has said of the ultimate and final resurrection, "Then shall come to pass the saying that is written, Death is swallowed up in victory" (v. 54). But I repeat, that is not so yet.

Death to humanity is always hostile and hateful. Of all the forces natural and spiritual, death is the least under human control. Life is far more under human control than is death. Death continues age after age, century after century, defying every attempt that man has made to discover its secret and to abolish it. We grant the benefits and the blessings that are ours in this age of scientific investigation and progress. But science has done nothing to deal with death. It has done much to alleviate pain, but not to deal with death. If for a moment we may be inclined to think that science has succeeded in postponing death when we think of the average length of human life in these days, we immediately discover that science has not been able to postpone death by a single hour. It cannot deal with it. We are still its slaves, its victims. It comes unexpectedly and in ways we never dreamed of, and even more terribly, sometimes with long advanced notice, it creeps upon us. We cannot buy death off or persuade it not to be; the human heart is naturally in revolt against it. Paul's word *echthros*, meaning "hateful, hostile, an enemy," is humanity's word, and Christianity has not attempted to change it. Here in a chapter that flashes with the light and glory of assured resurrection, the great apostle of Jesus Christ, filled with His Spirit and consumed with His life, breaks out into the language of my text, "The last *enemy* that shall be abolished is death."

Death is an enemy to this world. It is the wounder of hearts. It is the assailant of faith. it is the challenger of hope. It is the enemy of high and noble service, whether it be distinctively Christian or merely humanitarian. It stops the ear that was willing to listen to the tale of sorrow and to woe. It blinds the eyes that looked with love and sympathy and helpfulness upon those who were in need. It silences the lips that uttered words of comfort and praised the name of God. It fetters the feet that ran on errands of mercy. It paralyses the hands that delighted to serve. Come where or how it will, it is grim and ghastly. The Christian conception of release does not rob the earthly side of death of its terror. In the midst of the greatest passage in the Bible on the subject of the resurrection, the inspired writer speaks of death as an enemy.

This common consciousness of humanity, a consciousness born of the fact from which there can be no escape, is in itself an argument against the naturalness of death. Death is out of place in the life of man. There is no reason that can be discovered why a human spirit may not continue to reconstruct for itself, by the wonderful power of life, a tenement, a house. Why cannot this go on? Why is it that after a while there is a weakening of the process of reconstruction and the old buoyancy passes away? I affirm that science has no answer to my inquiry. Science will declare to me, after its perfectly proper and perfectly reverent investigation of phenomena, that death is the natural ending of life. I declare that science has no proof of its assertion. The riddle is solved by revelation only, and that in the statement, "The sting of death is sin" (v. 56). Death is the wage of sin. Not that the death of every individual is the result of the sin of that individual, for the saints of God are loosed from their sins, but they are not loosed from the pains of death. This is so because God has created, not a company of individuals but a race, the solidarity of which He maintains. Therefore men die as members of a race, even though under grace they may individually be redeemed from its curse.

Thus death persists, and man's hatred of it is part of his underlying and undestroyed relationship to the eternities. The protest of man against death is holy, for death remains an enemy. If it be objected that this is hardly the usual language of

Christianity about death, I again remind you that this is the language of the apostolic exclamation in the midst of his argument for resurrection. As the years pass on I have a growing sense of the hostility and the hatefulness of death.

But this is not all the text. The text refers to the abolition of death. Let us now consider what it means by that. Here at once we turn our faces toward the light, the essential Christian light. We unstop our ears that we may hear the distinctly Christian message. We hear this message nowhere else. No other religious system has this light. No human philosophy dare utter these words. It is the central and definite message of Christianity. Not even the Hebrew religion delivered it, nor could. The message that comes transfiguring death and enabling us to be strong even in the presence of our enemy, the message that declares the ultimate abolition of death, is not found in the Old Testament. There are gleams, hints, suggestions, inquiries. At last, through the processes of spiritual education, the people chosen of God rose to the conception of national immortality, but there was no final assurance of personal individual immortality. There is no real, final challenge to death in the Hebrew economy. This is distinctly Christian.

What, then, is the Christian teaching? First, that Christ has abolished death. This same apostle in his letter to Timothy wrote, "Our Saviour Jesus Christ, who abolished death, and brought life and immortality to light through the gospel" (2 Tim. 1:10). That Christ has abolished death is the central fact of Christianity. But, it may be said, Is not the Cross of Christ the central fact of Christianity? In some senses yes. Yet let me remind you, as I have often attempted to remind you, that apart from the resurrection the Cross of Christ is nothing other than a tragedy. Paul was surely right when he wrote in this chapter, "If Christ hath not been raised, then is our preaching vain, your faith also is vain" (1 Cor. 15:14). The Cross is vulgar, brutal, devilish, until, seeing it transfigured by the glory of the risen Christ, I am driven back to gaze once more upon the awful mystery. There I discover, shining out of the heart of the unfathomable darkness, the light that never was on land or sea in which men may walk even though they have sinned, and in the walking find themselves cleansed and made meet for the dwellings of the saints in light.

The resurrection is the central fact, and by this resurrection and all that it involves, Christ has abolished death. Let me say the simplest things that are in my heart in the simplest way I know. No true Christian believer should ever say that the life beyond, or rather the conception of the life beyond, is shrouded in mystery because no one has ever come back to tell us of its certainty. Yet how often have I heard this said by Christian men and women. Let me speak of them most tenderly. The thing is generally said when the heart is riven and bereft, bruised and desolate. Oh, if we might be sure, but no one has come back to tell us! But, surely in such speech, we forget that the central fact of Christianity is that Someone did come back from death to tell us of life. In that coming back, having died and risen from the dead, He abolished death—canceled it, as the word translated destroyed, or abolished, really means—rendered it useless, devoid of power. He paralyzed it, mastered it! Here is the central fact of our Christianity—Christ has abolished death in His own person by His resurrection. This is not only the central fact of Christian doctrine, it is proven true by the whole fact of Christianity. The proof that Christ rose is not merely that the fact is stated in these Scriptures of truth, the proof that Christ rose is the Church of Christ. By the Cross the men He had gathered around Him were driven from hope, from faith, if not from love. By the Cross the whole of His enterprise seemed to them to be ended. It was the fact that the Crucified rose that gathered back again the scattered, frightened disciples and held them in patient waiting until the strange and wonderful outpouring of the Divine Spirit filled them and illuminated the world as they were driven forth, the messengers of the Cross, the soldiers of the new crusade. The fact that gathered them together was the fact of the resurrection.

Thus in the presence of death we first of all affirm that Christ has abolished it in His own person, and by that abolition created His church. He created not merely His church as a body of Christian men and women believing and hoping in Him through the ages, but His church as the instrument of all the influences of right and purity and beauty, of cleansing and holiness, that have swept like rivers down two millenniums, slowly yet surely baptizing the nations into high ideals, and lifting men toward the full realization of the meaning of their lives. Whenever we come to the side of the grave, it is ours to set that grave in the light of the empty tomb in the garden of Joseph of Arimathea, and to feel that there beats upon its barren darkness the waves and billows of eternal light. Therefore while death remains an enemy, the resurrection stands confronting it, the resurrection of the Lord Himself, by which death is abolished.

That, however, is not all the truth. Christianity also teaches that the complete abolition of death is postponed. Until sin is cast out death cannot be cast out. "He must reign, till he hath put all his enemies under his feet. The last enemy that shall be abolished is death" (1 Cor. 15:25–26). In these words, the sequence of the campaign of Christ is suggested. He Himself, having abolished death in His own person, having appeared to those early disciples, and having constituted and formed His Christian church, now reigns. His reign is administrative, the application of the victory won personally, to all the affairs of human life and through all the centuries. The conflict goes forward against sin, against sorrow, against disease, against limitation, against all those things that blight and spoil humanity. Death cannot be abolished ultimately until these are abolished completely, not merely because death is the wage of sin, not merely because death is the outcome of sin but because death must be retained in the interest of those who sin and of those who suffer. Sin without death would be the cruelest fate that could overtake man. That is hell. Suffering without death would be the most brutal thing. Therefore man's natural death is retained until all other enemies have been subdued.

The light of this truth flashed and shone in the first pages of the Bible. God set at the gate of the garden of Eden a cherubim and a flaming sword, to guard the tree of life lest man should eat of the tree of life and live in sin forever. So in that hour, and through all the subsequent processes, death the enemy is made the minister of infinite justice against sin, and of release from the experience of suffering. But the risen Lord reigns over death. Death is no more outside His government than sin is outside His government, or suffering is outside His government. Death cannot come save by His permission. This is the Christian doctrine. To the man who has seen the risen Lord, and to the man who believes that the risen Christ reigns, the death that he hates, the death that is hostile, is nevertheless seen as held in leash, held in check, never permitted to advance or strike, save under His will and His government.

Reverently, therefore, let us now inquire finally, What is the true Christian spirit in the presence of the fact of death? What is the true Christian attitude toward the enemy, death?

The first fact we should recognize is that the true attitude of the Christian toward death is that of antagonism, conflict. We recognize that He reigns over it. But we recognize also that it still remains, and therefore that in cooperation with Him we are to be against it. There is to be no murder in any degree or under any circumstances. It is almost unnecessary to say in a Christian assembly that there must be no suicide. The Christian man cannot entertain the thought of it for a moment. I know right well that even to Christian souls there are times when it seems that such would be release, but Christianity demands the heroism that shall look upon death as an enemy and hold it off.

The Christian man must ever be in conflict with death by every method. By the observation of the laws of health and the employment of all medical science and skill, death is to be held away. Our attitude toward death must be that of perpetual antagonism.

Nevertheless in this strange and mysterious economy, over which our risen Lord is presiding and reigning, there are limits. Sooner or later death comes. What then is to be the Christian attitude toward its victory? It must be that of confidence. We must resolutely refuse to allow the physical in death to be the supreme thing in our consciousness. There must be in the presence of death the determined contemplation of all that is unseen to mortal eyes. We must always remind ourselves when we stand in the presence of our dead ones that the appearance upon which our eyes of sense are fixed is not all the fact. Just beyond the possibility of our human observation are realities definite and eternal. We must remember the fact of the spiritual. I stand by the side of my dead comrade. There he lies. Oh, but if I am a Christian man I must ever look through and beyond, and say to myself by the side of his coffin what the angel said of old in Joseph's garden, "he is risen; he is not here" (Mark 16:6)

Again confidence means assurance that the victory of death, even in the physical, is but for a little while. We must realize that the word is true to which we have listened in our hours of anguish, and yet have hardly heard for heaviness and sorrow of heart, the declaration that we lay the loved ones to rest in sure and certain hope of a glorious resurrection! Death has gained a victory for today. We are the poorer for it. Death is the enemy. But O death, your victory is but for a few short years! I know it is difficult, so very difficult to do this, for the years ahead look so long, so long! Yet it is for the Christian to live in God's *now*, expecting with the risen Christ—and He is expecting until His enemies including death be made the footstool of His feet—the dawning of that day when He shall have put down all rule and authority and all power, all that lift themselves against God, and when the very heart of God shall come to its ultimate gladness in the presence of humanity, as death is smitten unto death and ended forevermore. It is for us who claim to live in fellowship with God, to live expecting with Jesus. If we deny His resurrection, we are indeed of all men the most pitiable. The most pitiable of all, because the suggestion was so wonderful. If indeed it be a delusion, then in God's name we are of all men the most pitiable!

But we will not tarry there, but continue with the apostle and affirm, "But now hath Christ been raised from the dead" (1 Cor. 15:20). Because Christ has been raised from the dead, we say to death, You have gained your victory, oh enemy, but it will not be for long!

Finally, confidence in the presence of death means recognition of the fact that He reigns even over death. Therefore, much as we lose, the whole of His enterprise gains by every soul that passes over.

How much London has lost through the death of Thomas Nicholson. London is such a great Babylon that we hardly realize it; but that bereaved congregation realizes it! All the poetic beauty of that ministry, the wonderful insight and interpretation of the deep things of God is over. We suffer loss indeed!

How much the Five Towns have lost by the passing of a beautiful boy. God is helping us to see how much by the testimonies that are coming from far and near to the sweet and gracious influence exerted in office, athletic club, and among his friends everywhere. We have lost indeed! The Five Towns are poorer for the passing of Lennox Nutton.

There is loss in the city and loss in the town. But lift your eyes. The King has made no mistake. Jesus reigns in those spaces larger than these poor mortal eyes can gaze into. Thomas Nicholson and Lennie are serving the King, and the larger enterprises of God have gained by their passing. If you deny me that, then I am in revolt and rebellion against God! But you cannot deny me that. That is the song of my faith, the lamp of my hope, the joy of my heart!

When I went down to my friend in March, I sat and talked with this lad. He had begun to preach in the villages. I said to him, Lennie, "I hope to see you at Cheshunt some day." The boy did not answer me. He looked at me and I saw the light of wonder and hope in his eyes. And now I am inclined to say, It is all over! It is not all over! My judgment was inaccurate. I thought he might serve in a higher sphere than that in which he was occupied. But God has said to him that He needed him for a still higher sphere than I thought of. He has taken him.

Oh death, I hate you. But you are not master of the situation! You are the enemy, putting out the light of the eyes and sealing the ear, cruel enemy. But you are not king oh death. Jesus is King. The risen Lord and Master reigns. As the old Bishop put it, He has captured you and made you a porter at the gate of life! While we yet share in His sufferings in our losses, we will dare to rejoice in His gains, for in the ultimate, final economy, by every soul that passes over, God gains and the day of the last victory is hastened.

What then is to be our attitude in the presence of death? That of consolation which we receive from God and pass on to others. He is the God of all comfort, and He comforts us in our affliction that we may be able to comfort those who are also in affliction. Thus from the pain and sorrow of all bereaved hearts, there shall presently flow forth healing rivers for other wounded hearts. Wonderful, wonderful God! He lays upon me the burden and pain and bereavement in order that presently I may sit by another bereaved heart and help to heal it.

In the light of these things we lift up our heads. Those who are gone are with Christ. Those who are left have Christ with them. This is the true communion of saints. We have not lost our loved ones, save in the smallest sense. They are ours and we are theirs. God has them in His keeping until the morning without clouds shall break, and we shall meet to part no more in the land all sunlit, whence the night shades flee.

Vi Metcalf